Launch into Reading

THOMSON

HEINLE

Australia Canada Mexico Singapore Spain United Kingdom United States

THOMSON

™

HEINLE

Launch into Reading Student Book

Vice President, Editorial Director ESL: *Nancy Leonhardt*
Director of School Publishing: *Edward Lamprich*
Managing Developmental Editor: *Donna Schaffer*
Associate Developmental Editor: *Tania Maundrell-Brown*
Senior Production Editor: *Michael Burggren*
Manufacturing Manager: *Marcia Locke*
Director of Global ESL Training and Development: *Evelyn Nelson*
Marketing Manager: *Jim McDonough*
Editorial Assistant: *Elizabeth Allen*
Development, Design, and Production: *The GTS Companies*
Cover Illustrator: *David Diaz*
Cover Photograph (King Tut): *Charles & Josette Lenars/CORBIS*
Printer: *R.R. Donnelley and Sons Company, Willard*

Printed in the United States of America
3 4 5 6 7 8 9 10   06 05 04 03 02

ISBN: 0-8384-0112-0

For more information contact Heinle, 25 Thomson Place, Boston, Massachusetts 02210 USA,
or you can visit our Internet site at http://www.heinle.com

Dear Student

Welcome to *Launch into Reading*! There are three levels in this program. Each one will help you to read, write, listen, and speak effectively. Your textbook is divided into four units. There are four reading selections in each unit. The reading selections are related to each other by theme.

The readings in each unit are both fiction and nonfiction. Many well-known authors wrote these selections. Some of the readings are traditional and classic. Some of them are contemporary. We hope you enjoy reading them. At the end of each unit, you will find suggestions for other books to read.

There are helpful activities and strategies that go along with each reading. Before you read each selection, you will think about your own background and what you already know, then learn some new vocabulary words and find out how to use a reading strategy. As you read, you will get a chance to use the reading strategy. Your teacher will help you learn more about how to spell and sound out words. After you finish the reading, you will get a chance to show what you learned. You will connect what you learned to other classes that you are taking and to real life. You will also learn more about words, grammar, and writing.

As you use *Launch into Reading*, you will have a lot of support. Your *Student Workbook* and the *Student CD-ROM* will give you extra practice. At the end of each unit, you will be able to use everything you learned when you do the unit project. The projects are fun and will give you a chance to work with other students and use English outside of the classroom. You will also have a chance to work on the Internet.

We hope you have fun as you learn English with *Launch into Reading*. A whole world of possibilities awaits you!

Acknowledgments

Reviewers and Consultants

We want to thank our reviewers and consultants who made valuable contributions to *Launch into Reading.* The reviewers and consultants evaluated selections and provided advice on current pedagogy.

Consulting Author

Florence Decker has taught ESL in El Paso ISD and Dallas ISD, Texas. She has also conducted ESL methodology courses at the University of Texas in El Paso and at Centro de Lenguas in Juarez, Mexico. In addition, she has been involved in writing curricula for several school districts.

- **Donna Altes**
  Silverado Middle School
  Napa, California

- **Cally Andriotis-Williams**
  Newcomers High School
  Long Island City, New York

- **Lynn Clausen**
  Pajaro Valley Unified
  School District
  Watsonville, California

- **Mary Hadley**
  Georgia Southern University
  Statesboro, Georgia

- **Erik Johansen**
  Hueneme High School
  Oxnard, California

- **Cherylyn Smith**
  Fresno Unified School District
  Fresno, California

Contents

Launch
into
Reading

UNIT 1
Changes

"Nothing is permanent
but change."

—Heraclitus
(Greek philosopher, ca. 544–483 B.C.E.)

Discuss the Theme
Making Changes

Every day we make changes. Some changes are easy, such as changing clothes. Other changes, like moving to a new country, are harder and can affect everything in our lives. In this unit, you will read about a girl and her family who fled from war-torn Laos and ended up in the United States. You will read poems that call for a dramatic change in the way we live. You will learn about other changes in an article about how the ancient Egyptians prepared their dead for the next world. You will read a story about a boy who decides to make a big change in his life. Change can be difficult at first. But new, and often better, things come out of it.

- What easy changes have you made in the last week?
- What hard changes have you made in the last three years?
- Is it easy for you to make changes? Why or why not?
- What good things have happened because of changes you have made?

WRITING FOCUS:
Narrative

Before You Read

Background

What do you know about your family's history? Where did your family come from? A personal history of a family is an important way to keep memories alive. In this autobiographical narrative, the author tells the story of her journey to the United States.

Dia's Story Cloth

an autobiographical narrative by Dia Cha

LEARNING OBJECTIVES

- Use notes, outlines, and summaries
- Understand complete sentences
- Recognize words from other languages used in English
- Establish and develop plot

Building Your Vocabulary

1. This reading describes the lives of people who spend much of their lives working on the land and preparing food. Their lives change when a war starts. On a separate sheet of paper, draw a chart like the one you see on page 5. Then, sort the following words into two categories: **Village Life** or **War.**

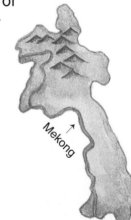

Mekong

Reading: Classify categories of words

highlands	jungles	banana leaves
bamboo	barracks	recruited
bombs	guerrillas	harvest

Village Life	War
bamboo	*barracks*

2. Compare your chart with a partner's. Use a dictionary to look up words you don't know.

Reading Strategy

Notes, outlines, and summaries Taking notes helps you remember a lot of facts when you read nonfiction. Outlining helps organize facts. Writing summaries helps you understand the facts.

Applying the Reading Strategy

1. As you read, write down the important ideas.

2. After you have written your notes, organize them in an outline by listing the main ideas in order.

Once you have your main ideas, list details that support them.

3. Once you have an outline, use it to write a summary of the reading. A summary takes the ideas in the outline and ties them together in paragraphs.

As you read "Dia's Story Cloth," take notes on the main ideas. Write down any supporting details.

Reading: Clarify an understanding of text by creating notes, outlines, and summaries

Dia's Story Cloth

an autobiographical narrative by Dia Cha

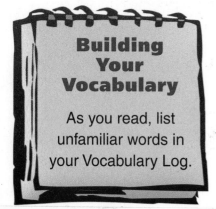

ancient / able
wanted / wished
would / wood
Foot / thatched
arrived / Palm
settled / leaves
build / wanked
daily / Dia's
Fields / pound, walked harvest
tended the crops / Filled, growing
tools / Peaceful
carried
Kinds
baskets
backs

As You Read

1. What does the word **ancestors** mean? Why did the author's ancestors **migrate,** or leave their homeland?

2. Where do her ancestors go? What do they do every day?

A long time ago, my ancestors lived in China. The ancient Chinese government wanted to change the way the Hmong lived. But my people would not give up their culture, and fled on foot across the river and through jungles to southeast Asia. Some went to Burma; some went to Thailand. Like many Hmong, my ancestors migrated to Laos.

When they arrived in Laos, the Hmong settled in the tropical highlands where no one had lived before. They had to clear forests to build their villages and plant their crops. They grew corn and rice.

The daily life in the Hmong villages included working in the fields from morning to night. Both men and women tended the crops. Everything from tools to food was carried in different kinds of baskets on their backs.

In Laos, the Hmong were able to farm as they wished and lived in peace for many years.

When I was a child, in the 1960s, my family lived in a wood and bamboo house with a thatched roof made of palm leaves. Every morning I helped my mother and sisters pound rice. After breakfast, my family walked for almost two hours to our mountainside fields, where we worked all day. Every evening we walked back home. At harvest time we each carried a backpack basket filled with rice or corn.

But as I was growing up, the peaceful life of my village was disappearing.

Laos was caught in warfare. My country was divided in two: On one side, many Hmong men

Reading: Use context to find the meaning of unknown words

joined the loyalist army, which was su[pported]
by the American government. On the [other]
side was the communist regime, which
also recruited many Hmong men.

My father left to fight with the
loyalist troops. My family began
to move from village to village to
escape the communist soldiers.

Communist soldiers came to
the Hmong villages and
captured the men. They tied
the Hmongs' hands behind
their backs and took them
away. The Hmong men kneeled
down and begged for their lives,
but the soldiers didn't listen.
The Hmong women couldn't do
anything to help. They cried and
cried because they knew they might
never see their husbands and sons
again.

My father was sent to fight in Xieng
Khuang province. He never came back. We
don't know whether he was killed or captured.
Airplanes dropped bombs on the Hmong villages.
Many houses were destroyed by flames. Women
and children fled into the jungle and lived in huts
made from banana leaves. I remember having to
get up in the middle of the night, feeling so afraid
because we had to flee our hiding place.
Sometimes we hid in the forest, or in caves until
the communist soldiers left.

BURMA
LAOS
THAILAND
CAMBODIA
MEKONG
RIVER

As You Read

1. Look over your notes.
   What main ideas or
   facts have you written
   down so far?

2. Based on your notes,
   what do you think
   happened?

loyalist: someone who is faithful to his or her country's government
province: an administrative area of a country

The Vietnamese war took place in Vietnam, but affected all of Southeast Asia. Supporters of the existing government and the Communist Party fought against each other. The United States entered the war to try to stop the spread of communism in Southeast Asia.

As You Read

1. What are the main ideas and facts about the author's life in the United States?

2. What part of the story have you written most about so far? Why?

The communist soldiers shot at the Hmong men. The guerrilla soldiers came from their camps in the jungle and shot at the communists.

Many people died.

In 1975 the Americans pulled out of Laos, and the communist regime took over. My mother was determined to get us out of Laos. I was 10 years old when we fled.

Escaping meant we had to cross the Mekong River. But the river was dangerous. People who didn't have boats had to cross by swimming or using inner tubes and bamboo poles to stay afloat. Many people died trying to cross this river.

Like other escaping Hmong, we lived in a refugee camp when we arrived in Thailand. We lived in barracks. Some families planted small gardens. All the Hmong were very homesick.

Earlier in Laos, my mother had destroyed all the documents we had relating to my father and the war. So we didn't have anything to prove my father was actually fighting on the side of the Americans. But when we got to the camp, one of my father's friends gave us a photo of my father taken at the front lines.

The U.S. government sent staff to interview the Hmong refugees to determine who would be able to emigrate to America. When the American lady came to interview us, the photo of my father was our proof that we were qualified as political refugees. In 1979, after four and a half years in the camp, we left Thailand for America.

As the buses left the camp, we said goodbye to all the people we knew. In some families there were members who had to stay behind in

guerrilla: a member of an independent group of soldiers

Reading: Distinguish the main idea

Thailand, while their relatives were allowed to go to America. Many people cried.

When my people first arrived in America, most didn't speak or write English. Many families had sponsors, who picked us up at the airport.

Everything about life in America was different for the Hmong.

I was 15 years old when I came to this country. I'd never been to school, so I had to start everything from scratch. They wanted to put me in high school, but I didn't know anything. Then they wanted to put me in an adult school, but the teachers said I was too young.

Finally, I started high school. Thirteen years later, I received my master's degree from Northern Arizona University. I went back to Laos as an anthropologist in 1992 to work with Hmong and Lao women in the refugee camps in Thailand.

A b o u t   t h e   A u t h o r

Dia Cha

Dia Cha was born in Laos. In 1975 she and her family fled Laos and went to Thailand. They spent more than four years in a refugee camp there before they were able to come to the United States. Dia Cha became one of the first Hmong American women to get an advanced degree. *Dia's Story Cloth* is her first book for young readers.

anthropologist: a scientist who studies people and societies

Retell It!

Compare the notes you took with those of your classmates. Where do you think they will fit in an outline? Work together to create an outline for "Dia's Story Cloth," using the facts in your notes. Go back to the reading to look for other facts.

Think, Discuss, Write

In your group, discuss your answers to these questions. Write your answers on a separate sheet of paper.

1. **Analyze plot**   What year did Dia and her family leave Thailand and go to the United States? What did she do there?

2. **Recognize cause and effect**   Why did the Hmong people leave China and go to Laos?

3. **Analyze cause and effect**   Why did the author's family leave Laos for the United States?

4. **Connect recurring themes**   How would life in the United States be different from life in Laos?

5. **Connect recurring themes**   Would it be difficult or easy for the Hmong people to begin new lives in the United States? Why?

6. **Compare and contrast**   Your outline tells the story of Dia's journey from Laos. Dia's aunt and uncle made a story cloth that tells the same story with pictures. How are the two ways of telling the story the same?

7. **Compare and contrast**   How are the two ways of telling the story different?

Reading: Retell the central ideas of simple passages

What's Your Opinion?

Could you go through what the Hmong people did? On a separate sheet of paper, copy the sentences and put a **1** next to the things that would be very hard or frightening. Put a **2** next to things that might also be encouraging.

- Hide in caves from soldiers
- Cross the Mekong River to get out of Laos
- Raise food in a garden in a refugee camp
- Leave the refugee camp to live in the United States

Launch into Grammar

Complete sentences A **complete sentence** has **a subject,** which is the topic of the sentence, and a **verb,** which describes the action. The subject and verb of a sentence must **agree.** If the subject is singular, the verb must be singular. If the subject is plural, the verb must be plural.

Singular: She helps her mother pound rice.
Plural: Their parents live in China.

   With a partner, find three examples of complete sentences in the reading that have singular subjects. Then find three examples of complete sentences with plural subjects.

 For more practice with complete sentences, use page 3 of the Student Workbook.

Written conventions: Identify subjects and verbs that are in agreement

Launch into Word Analysis

Word origins   English borrows words from other languages. You can get a good idea of what these words mean from **context.** (Context means the other words and sentences that appear with that word in the reading.)

   "Dia's Story Cloth" has words borrowed from different languages. Copy the chart below on a separate piece of paper. Match words on the left with their definitions on the right. Then guess which language these words come from.

 For more practice with words that are borrowed in English, complete page 4 of the Student Workbook.

Bamboo.

Words	Definition	Language
1. regime	a. type of plant with hollow stems	• French
2. guerrilla	b. person who must leave his or her country to seek protection	• Spanish
3. bamboo	c. government or ruling power	• French
4. refugee	d. soldier who fights outside an army	• Chinese

Reading: Recognize the origins and meanings of frequently used foreign words and use these words accurately in speaking and writing

Launch into Writing

Plot   What happens in Dia's story is called the **plot.** The plot in any story has five elements: *exposition* (background), *rising action, climax, falling action,* and *resolution.*

On a separate sheet of paper, make a short list of important events in your life. Here is an example of a list you might make:

When I moved.
When I started a new school.
When my sister left home.

Choose one event and circle it. Suppose you are going to tell a story about this event. What would be the plot elements in your story? Beneath your list, write the five plot elements. Then write ideas for each element in your story. When you finish, exchange papers with a partner to check your plot elements. Use this example to help you:

exposition (background)	My oldest sister and I used to share a room.
rising action	I didn't want her to leave home. I knew she would.
climax	She finally moved. I was really sad.
falling action	I went to visit her last month.
resolution	I spent the night in her new room. It was like sharing a room again.

For more practice with plot development, complete pages 6–7 of the Student Workbook.

The Hmong people who came to the United States in the late 1970s and early 1980s were used to a rural life of farming. However, their skill at sewing allowed many of them to find work as tailors. People who like folk art greatly value Hmong tapestries.

A Hmong story cloth.

Dia's Story Cloth   13

2

1. Angels Ride Bikes

and

2. Angels Ride Bikes

by Francisco X. Alarcón

Before You Read

Background

When you think of your home, your school, and your community, can you think of things you would like to change? What would you keep the same? What would you do to make your world a better place? The two poems in this chapter may give you some idea of where to start.

LEARNING OBJECTIVES

- Identify and analyze different types of fiction
- Understand interrogatives
- Identify and understand figurative language
- Establish setting

Building Your Vocabulary

1. What does the word **community** mean to you? Are you part of a community?

2. Look at the diagram below. It shows different words from the poems. What title can you give to each group of words?

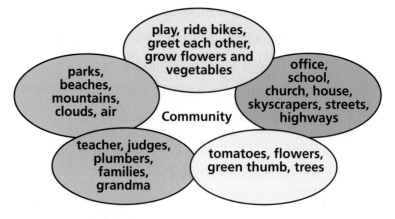

play, ride bikes, greet each other, grow flowers and vegetables

parks, beaches, mountains, clouds, air

office, school, church, house, skyscrapers, streets, highways

Community

teacher, judges, plumbers, families, grandma

tomatoes, flowers, green thumb, trees

Reading: Classify categories of words

Reading Strategy

Identify and analyze different types of fiction

Fiction is writing that tells a story. Fiction includes any kind of writing that is imaginary, or not based on facts. Short stories and novels are fiction. Poems and plays can also be fictional. Each type of fiction has its own special features. When you read fiction, be sure to identify the type of fiction you are reading and look for its special features. These special features will help you understand and enjoy the story.

Applying the Reading Strategy

1. When you read a short story or novel, look for the characters and plot to be introduced in paragraphs. A short story captures an event or moment in a single, brief chapter. A novel usually looks at characters and plot in many chapters over a longer, more drawn-out period of time.

2. Instead of paragraphs, a play uses blocks of dialogue (characters' words) to tell a story. Plays are written to be performed by actors on stage.

3. Poetry is the most open and imaginative way to tell a story. Instead of paragraphs or blocks of text, poems are often written in verses. A poem is usually short. It may rhyme, have a strong rhythm, and use vivid images to capture the reader's attention.

4. When you read a poem, be prepared to use your imagination. Listen to how the poem sounds to your ear. Let the poem's word images form pictures in your mind. Be flexible. Let the meaning of the poem come to you. When in doubt, read the poem again.

You are going to read two poems. Look at the form of each poem first. How long is the poem? How many verses does it have? How are the verses arranged on the page? As you read, remember to use your imagination.

Reading: Identify the forms of fiction and describe the major characteristics of each form

Angels Ride Bikes

poems by Francisco X. Alarcón

1. our teacher
Miss Baker
somberly tells us:

"today
we can't go
outside to play

there's too much
smog that's harmful
to our health"

from a window
I look at the dirty
gray air

I imagine
trees crying
in distress

and dogs
beginning
to cough

I beg
the heavens
for a signal

2. suddenly
I see bicycles
everywhere

bicycles
in parks
and beaches

bicycles
on streets
and highways

I see judges
and plumbers
on bikes

entire
families
on bikes

the whole
city riding
on bikes

once again
the air turns
pure and clean

I can see
the skyscrapers
the mountains

and on a cloud
I see my grandma
on her bicycle

among
the angels
riding bikes

As You Read

1. In the first poem, what does the speaker see through the classroom window?

2. What kinds of people are riding bikes in the second poem?

Reading: Identify the forms of fiction

Los ángeles andan en bicicleta

poemas de Francisco X. Alarcón

1. nuestra maestra
Miss Baker
nos dice sombría:

"hoy no podemos
salir afuera
a jugar

hay demasiado
smog dañino
a la salud"

por una ventana
miro el aire
sucio y gris

me imagino
a los árboles
llorar

a los perros
empezar
a toser

al cielo
le suplico
una señal

2. de pronto
por dondequiera
veo bicicletas

bicicletas
en los parques
y las playas

bicicletas
por las calles
y las carreteras

veo a jueces
y plomeros
en bicicleta

a familias
enteras
en bicicleta

la ciudad
toda anda
en bicicleta

el aire es
otra vez
puro y limpio

distingo
los rascacielos
las montañas

y en una nube
veo a mi abuela
en su bici

entre los ángeles
que andan
en bicicleta

About the Author

Francisco X. Alarcón

Francisco X. Alarcón is the award-winning author of many collections of poetry. He lives in Davis, California, and is the director of the Spanish for Native Speakers program at the University of California. He is considered a leader of the Chicano literary movement. He writes in both Spanish and English.

After You Read

The word **Chicano** can be used to refer to Mexican Americans. Many Chicanos are the sons and daughters of Mexicans but were born and live in the United States. Many, but not all, Chicanos speak Spanish.

Retell It!

Both of these poems seem to make a statement about the environment. What statement do they make? Summarize the message of the poems in your own words.

Think, Discuss, Write

1. **Recall details**   What does Miss Baker tell the class in the first poem?

2. **Describe**   What unusual images does the author present of trees and a dog in the first poem?

3. **Plot**   What problem or conflict does the author face in both poems? How does he solve this problem?

4. **Describe**   What special images does the author present in the second poem? What causes these images to appear?

5. **Compare and contrast**   Compare and contrast the images that the author creates in the poems. Which image paints the most vivid picture in your mind?

6. **Draw a conclusion**   What point do you think the author is trying to make in his poems?

7. **Analyze**   How do the images in the poems help the author make his point? Explain and give examples.

Reading: Extract information from the text, including problems and solutions

What's Your Opinion?

The author thinks that riding bikes would help the environment. What do you think? Is this a good way to help the environment? If so, why?

What other things can you think of that would help the environment? Make a list of them. Here are a few ideas.

- Planting trees
- Turning off lights when you don't need them
- Making less trash
- Driving smaller cars
- Walking instead of driving
- Turning off air conditioners

Launch into Grammar

Interrogatives and declaratives A simple sentence can ask a question. Sentences that ask questions are called interrogative sentences. Interrogative sentences often begin with words like **who, what, when, where, how,** or **why**. Interrogatives can also be formed by placing the verb before the subject. A question mark comes at the end of an interrogative sentence.

Written conventions: Understand and be able to use interrogative sentences

Sentences that make statements are called declaratives.

Example:

Declarative sentence: We can go outside to play.
Interrogative sentence: When can we go outside to play? Can we go outside to play?

With a partner, find five declarative sentences from the reading. Make them interrogative using **who, what, when, where,** or **why** as in the example above. Then make them interrogative by placing the verb before the subject.

 For more practice with interrogatives and declaratives, use page 11 of the Student Workbook.

Launch into Word Analysis

Figurative language   Figurative language makes creative comparisons between ideas or things. For example, in the poem " 2. Angels Ride Bikes," the poet compares people who ride bicycles to angels. Work in a small group. On a separate sheet of paper, copy the following examples of figurative language. Match each example on the left with what it means on the right.

1. He eats like a horse.
2. He eats like a bird.
3. That suit fits like a glove.
4. That suit is as big as a barn.
5. She has eyes like an eagle.

a. That suit fits well.
b. He eats a lot.
c. That suit is too large.
d. She sees very well.
e. He does not eat much.

Reading: Identify and interpret figurative language;
Written conventions: Distinguish between declarative and interrogative sentences

For more practice with figurative language, complete page 12 of the Student Workbook.

Launch into Writing

Establish setting Writers use **sensory details** and **concrete language** to establish the setting in a poem. Sensory details are words that show how things look, feel, taste, smell, and sound. Concrete language describes things accurately and tells the reader exactly what the writer has in mind.

Sensory details: We heard the scream of sirens as the cherry-red fire truck roared by.

Concrete language: The thin cotton sheet was folded crisply into a neat, three-cornered shape.

Write a paragraph on a separate sheet of paper about a place that has special meaning to you. Use sensory details and concrete language to make your description come to life.

 For more practice with sensory details and concrete language, use pages 14–15 of the Student Workbook.

Writing: Include sensory details and concrete language to develop plot and character

3

Before You Read

Background

Death can be the most difficult change of all to accept. Most cultures have traditions that help people accept death. In this nonfiction article, you will learn what the ancient Egyptians believed about death and the afterlife. You will also find out how they prepared the bodies of the dead for the next world. Then you will get to try something similar with a potato!

DEATH and the
AFTERLIFE

**an excerpt from a
nonfiction book by
Judith Crosher**

Recipe
for a Mummy

**an excerpt from a
nonfiction book
by Vicki Cobb and
Kathy Darling**

LEARNING OBJECTIVES

- Follow steps in a process
- Understand imperatives
- Understand and use hyphenated words
- Describe a process with sequence words

Building Your Vocabulary

The nonfiction excerpts you are about to read contain several unfamiliar words. Some of these words can be found in a dictionary. Others can be defined only by reading the selection itself.

    With a partner, copy the table on page 23 and

Reading: Monitor text for unknown words

place the words from the story into one of the two columns.

Use a dictionary to look up the words you put in the first column. Move the words to the correct column if needed. Check these meanings later when you read the selection.

ka   cavity   natron
akh   Anubis   incision
sprigs   linen   Yalu
embalmed   mummify   securely

Probably in the dictionary	Probably not in the dictionary
linen	*ka*

Reading Strategy

Follow steps in a process   The two excerpts you are about to read describe processes. Whenever you make something, like cooking your favorite meal or even writing a story, you do several small things one after the other. The order in which you do these steps is as important as the steps themselves, if you want what you make to turn out right! The order in which you do something is called a **process.**

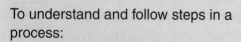

Applying the Reading Strategy

To understand and follow steps in a process:

1. Reread the first paragraph and determine what the author is trying to tell you. As you read the first paragraph, ask yourself: What is the most important thing for me to remember?

2. As you continue reading, ask yourself: What is the goal of this process? How does each step contribute something to this goal?

3. Reread each paragraph of the reading and note the main ideas.

4. Think about how these main ideas fit together as you try to understand what the reading is about.

Reading: Identify structural patterns found in informational text

DEATH and the AFTERLIFE

**an excerpt from a nonfiction book
by Judith Crosher**

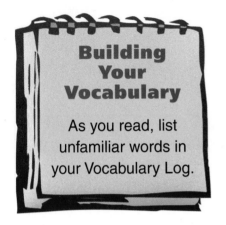

Building Your Vocabulary

As you read, list unfamiliar words in your Vocabulary Log.

The ancient Egyptians believed that everyone had several parts: the ka, or spiritual double, created at birth and released from the body at death; the ba, or soul; and the akh, or super-natural power. As long as the body was preserved, the ka and ba would live. This is why it was thought to be so important to be properly mummified and laid in a tomb where offerings of food could be made, which would nourish the ka.

Preparing the mummy

In a tent called the "Beautiful House," near a temple, priests laid the body on a long, narrow table. The priest first pushed an instrument up the nostril and into the brain (thought to be worthless), and pulled it out in bits. Then he cleaned the mouth and filled it with sweet-oil-scented linen.

A priest in a mask of Anubis (the jackal-headed god of embalming) drew a line down the flank of the corpse, and a man came in, cut the incision, and was chased out with curses, for it was forbidden to injure an Egyptian. The priest removed the internal organs, putting back the precious heart, and filled the cavity with bags of natron (a drying mixture of salt, sodium bicarbonate, and sodium carbonate) and sweet-smelling gums. The body and the organs were covered with

flank: the side of a person between the ribs and the thigh

Reading: Use context to find the meaning of unknown words

natron and left on a sloping table for 40 days, until they were completely dry.

The internal organs were placed in four containers called canopic jars, after being treated in the same way as the mummy and wrapped in linen. The stoppers of the jars were carved to represent four minor gods called the Sons of Horus. Imsety, the human-headed god, looked after the liver; Hapy, the ape-headed god, the lungs; Duamutef, the jackal-headed god, the stomach; and Qebehsenuef, the hawk-headed god, the intestines. The jars were placed in the tomb with the mummy.

The priests sewed up the incision, rubbed the body with cedar oil, and filled the eye sockets with onions or white painted stones. Finally, they put in stuffings of spices and linen to replace the internal organs of the body, and began to wrap it.

Wrapping the body

The body was wrapped with up to 150 yards of linen, sometimes old sheets, or special cloths given by the temple, once an old torn up sail. About 100 amulets (protective charms) were placed inside the bandages to strengthen different parts of the body. The most important were the heart scarab, which meant rebirth, the djed pillar for strength, and the eye of Horus for restoring health. Sprigs of rosemary and flower bulbs were also put

djed pillar: a hieroglyphical symbol meaning stability

As You Read

1. What are the three parts of each person, according to the Egyptians?

2. Which two of these three parts would live after death if the body was preserved?

3. Who is the person mainly involved in the preparation of the body?

As You Read

1. How many crimes is the *akh* judged against? Who is the main judge?

2. What is the Gobbler? What does it do?

3. If a person's *akh* passes judgment, where does it go?

inside the bandages, sometimes even pets. One girl had her pet monkey mummified and wrapped with her. An onion, for health, was put in the mummy's hand. At each stage prayers were said. Finally, the mummy was painted with resin , a mask was put over its face, and it was put into a coffin painted with the person's portrait so that its ka would recognize it in the afterlife.

Judgment time

Once in the tomb, it was believed that the akh began its journey to the hall of judgment. There it was judged against a list of 42 crimes. The god Anubis held the scales . The person's heart lay in one pan, in the other the feather of Ma'at, Goddess of Justice. The more crimes the dead person admitted to, the heavier the heart. If it outweighed the feather, then the Gobbler, a monster made of lion, crocodile, and hippo, swallowed it, and it became an evil spirit, forever fighting the gods. If it passed the test, it went with Osiris to live in the fields of Yalu, a place like Egypt though more beautiful.

resin: a gummy plant substance used to bind things together
scale: a tool used to measure weight

About the Author

Judith Crosher

Judith Crosher, author of "Death and the Afterlife" from *Ancient Egypt*, is a second-grade teacher in England. She has written about ancient civilizations for young readers.

Reading: Demonstrate comprehension by identifying answers in the text

Recipe for a Mummy

an excerpt from a nonfiction book by Vicki Cobb and Kathy Darling

Immortalize a piece of potato for future viewing (not eating).
Where: Yard
Special Conditions: Nice weather

Doing the Deed

Traditionally, a mummy is a dead body, human or animal, that has been preserved. Breaking with tradition, you can make a *vegetable* mummy. This recipe for creating a potato mummy is almost exactly like the one used by the ancient Egyptians to mummify bodies. It will keep bacteria from rotting the vegetable remains.

You will need:
½ cup baking soda
½ cup washing soda (found in the detergent section of the supermarket)
¼ cup salt
a plastic cup
a spoon
a slice of potato
plastic wrap

Mix the baking soda, washing soda, and salt together in the plastic cup, using the spoon. Then lay the slice of potato to rest in the plastic cup "tomb." Cover the cup securely with the plastic wrap. Bury the future mummy in the ground.

immortalize: to give something eternal life

Connecting to History

The ancient Egyptians created a great civilization along the banks of the Nile River around 3000 B.C. Their religious beliefs inspired them to create a complex life full of rituals and traditions. They built the giant pyramids to honor their dead and protect their mummies.

To make this more scientific, cut two more slices of potato. Bury one beside your embalmed specimen. Place the other on the surface of the ground.

Wait ten days. Then examine all your potato slices for signs of rot and decay.

Insider Information
Mummification is an amazing method of preservation that has been used by humans for four or five thousand years. It also occurs naturally, through freezing, drying, or preservation in peat bogs or oil seeps. Some natural mummies are more than twenty-five thousand years old. The Egyptians practiced artificial mummification. They removed the body fluids with a kind of washing soda called *natron*. Then they put herbs and spices into the body before it was wrapped in linen. The process took seventy days.

Water is contained in every cell of every living thing and removing it without damaging the body is not easy. But it can be drawn out chemically with salts. Washing soda, baking

As You Read

1. How long have humans used the method of mummification?

2. What are three ways that mummification happens naturally?

specimen: a material used for testing or study

Reading: Follow multi-step instructions

soda, and table salt are all part of the group of chemicals known as salts. Why would you want to remove water from the body? Bacteria that cause decay cannot grow where there is no water.

So Tater Tut is now officially a mummy. *Caution!* Raccoons are known to be hazardous to the survival of potato mummies. Our neighborhood raccoons are notorious grave robbers.

tater: a potato

About the Authors

Vicki Cobb and Kathy Darling are the authors of *Don't Try This at Home! Science Fun for Kids on the Go*, which includes "Recipe for a Mummy."

Vicki Cobb

Vicki Cobb has a bachelor's degree in zoology from Barnard College and a master's degree in secondary science education from Columbia University.

Kathy Darling

Kathy Darling has a bachelor's degree in biochemistry from Russell Sage College. She has lived in more than thirty countries and is the author of several books on animal life cycles.

After You Read

Retell It!

The ancient Egyptians used picture-writing, or hieroglyphics, as a writing system. Retell the selections you just read using your own form of picture-writing. Retell the stories using pictures, symbols, or diagrams.

Think, Discuss, Write

In small groups, discuss your answers to these questions.

1. **Recall details**   Why was preserving a person's body important to the ancient Egyptians?

2. **Describe**   What steps did the priests take to prepare a body? Why weren't they allowed to cut the body?

3. **Compare and contrast**   How were the methods described in these readings of preserving a mummy and the potato similar? How were they different?

4. **Identify**   What sources could you use to find out more about main ideas that appeared in either of these articles?

5. **Infer**   Bacteria will rot any once-living thing. How did the steps taken to create the "mummy" potato prevent bacteria from growing?

6. **Draw a conclusion**   What happened in the Egyptian hall of judgment? How might the judgment process have encouraged Egyptians to be good people while they were alive?

Connecting to Science

When you study science, you often do **experiments.** Experiments are used to test ideas. The experiment you did in *Recipe for a Mummy* is a **chemical** experiment. Chemistry is one branch of science. Other branches are biology, physics, and zoology.

Reading: Ask questions and support answers by connecting prior knowledge with information from the text

7. Predict What do you expect to find when you examine your potatoes ten days from now?

What's Your Opinion?

Mummies were sacred to the ancient Egyptians. Yet, mummies were used to make wrapping paper in 19th century America. Do people have a right to use sacred objects from the past in whatever way they like? Voice how you feel on this topic.

Launch into Grammar

Imperatives An imperative is a verb that gives a command or makes a request.

Examples: Get your bike.
Clean up your room.

With your partner, skim the recipe and find four examples of imperatives, or sentences that give a command.

For more practice with imperatives, complete page 19 of the Student Workbook.

Written conventions: Understand and be able to use imperative sentences

Launch into Word Analysis

Hyphenated words   Hyphenated words are two or more separate words that are joined by a hyphen. When words are hyphenated, it means that *all* of those words are necessary to understand the meaning of the hyphenated word. You may know what each word means by itself, but they can take on a new meaning when joined together. For instance, "Recipe for a Mummy" contains the word **sweet-oil-scented.** All of these words go together to create one, more specific, hyphenated word.

With a partner, create some new hyphenated words. On a separate sheet of paper, using the information given on the next page, rewrite each sentence, using the hyphenated word you created. The example on the next page will help you.

> **Example:**   Anubis was a god **with the head of a jackal.**
>
> Anubis was a jackal-headed god.

1. The Gobbler was a monster **with the head of a lion.**

2. Bitumen is a substance **like tar.**

3. The cavity was filled with gums **which smelled sweet.**

 For more practice with hyphenated words, use page 20 of the Student Workbook.

Reading: Read and create hyphenated words

Launch into Writing

Describe a process with sequence words

Writers often use sequence words to describe a process or give instructions. These words tell when things should happen in a process. Examples of sequence words are *first, next, then, as soon as,* and *finally*. Think about a time when you told someone how to do something. Make a list of the instructions you gave that person. Now write the instruction in a paragraph, using sequence words. Here is an example:

> Cut a potato.
> Bury it in the ground.
> Wait ten days.
> Examine the slices for signs of decay.

> First, cut a potato. Next, bury it in the ground and wait ten days. Then examine the slices for signs of decay.

 For more practice with describing a process with sequence words, complete pages 22–23 of the Student Workbook.

Writing: Use sequence words when writing

4

Before You Read

**THE
GREAT
TURKEY WALK**

an excerpt from a novel
by Kathleen Karr

Background

Making changes can be risky. But sometimes people "take the plunge" and try something that they have never done before. Simon Green is one such person. Simon has recently "graduated" from school and is now ready to make a change and strike out on his own. Simon gets a good idea to earn a lot of money selling turkeys—but does someone so young and "pea-brained" (Simon's own word) have the ability to carry out such a bold plan? Find out in the excerpt from Kathleen Karr's *The Great Turkey Walk.*

LEARNING OBJECTIVES

- Analyze the way characters affect the plot in a piece of fiction
- Make verbs agree with subjects
- Understand colloquial English
- Write dialogue

Building Your Vocabulary

The Great Turkey Walk is set in eastern Missouri in 1860. Because it is told in language that was used a hundred years ago, some words will be new to you. Other

Reading: Use context to find the meaning of unknown words

words are more common today but they are special words for farming or school. With a partner, look at the list of words. What are they related to? Draw a picture like the one on the right, and put the words in the place they fit best—the barn or the school.

schoolmarm   decimal point   mules   foals

graduated   scrap of paper   flock   turkeys

Reading Strategy

Analyze the effect of character on plot   The character traits of people in a story can affect the **plot,** or the events that happen in a story. For example, a friendly character will not take the same course of action in a story that an unfriendly character takes. In a similar way, a hard-working character will make different choices in a story than a character who likes to avoid hard work. These choices will have a major effect on the plot of the story and how it is resolved.

Applying the Reading Strategy

1. As you read, ask yourself: What character traits does Simon have? Is he: honest? stubborn? shy? hard-working? Is he really as "pea-brained" as he claims to be? Make a list of Simon's character traits as you read.

2. As you read, keep track of the important events in the plot. Then look for links between plot events and character traits. For example, Simon seems to be a fairly determined young man. How does his determination affect his ability to "sell" his plan to Miss Rogers?

3. As you read, think about how the plot might have changed had Simon been someone with different character traits. How might the plot have changed had he been less determined to get things done?

The Great Turkey Walk   35

THE GREAT TURKEY WALK

an excerpt from a novel by Kathleen Karr

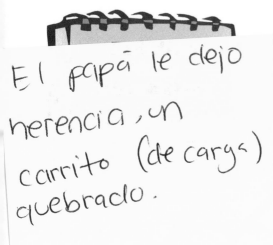

El papá le dejo herencia, un carrito (de carga) quebrado.

As You Read

1. Why does Uncle Lucas let Simon have the wagon?
2. Why does Simon live with his aunt and uncle?
3. How do Simon's cousins treat him?

I forked three big pork chops onto my plate at dinner that night. "Pass the potatoes, Cousin Ned." A mountain of mashed potatoes joined my chops. I drowned it all in thick gravy. Shoveled in a bite.

"Uncle Lucas?"

"Eh? Can't hear you for the mashies, Simon."

I swallowed and waited on my next bite, famished though I was. "Know that old wagon falling apart behind the barn?"

"What of it?"

"If I was to fix it up, could I have it?"

Uncle Lucas grunted. Cousins Ned, Homer, Pete, and Marcus stared at me over their own heaping plates with their beady little eyes. They was probably figuring on what part of their inheritance that old broken-down wagon was. Aunt Maybelle, at the bottom of the table, took an interest, too.

"What you want with that old wreck, Simon?" she asked.

I shoveled in another bite, considering. Finally spit out the news. "Got me graduated from school today. Fixing on setting up in business."

Their blank looks turned devious. Each and every one of 'em.

"On my own," I added. I sank my teeth into a chop to let them digest that.

Aunt Maybelle dabbed her apron at a corner of her eye. "You'll be leaving us, Simon? After all these years?"

"God willing, Aunt Maybelle."

Uncle Lucas downed a draft of his cider.

inheritance: something received from a relative when he or she dies

Reading: Distinguish facts, supported inferences, and opinions in text

"Supposin' you was to fix that old wagon." He stopped. "Supposin' I was to give it to you. Out of the kindness of my heart, as a sort of inheritance. In memory of my dear sister Samantha—God rest her soul—departed these ten long years—"

"Sure as shooting not in memory of her good-for-nothing husband, Samson, departed—but not to his just rewards—these same ten long years!"

Aunt Maybelle just had to tack that on. She'd done so with regularity over those aforementioned years. Always made me wonder about the pa I couldn't hardly remember. I laid down a bare bone and set to with another chop.

"Just supposin' . . ." Uncle Lucas peered at me. "What you figure pullin' it with?"

"Mules," I answered promptly. "My four mules that I hand-fed from foals, when their mamas give up on them."

Well, that started a row.

"Pa!" yelled Cousin Homer. "Since when's those mules Simon's?"

"Just 'cause they won't do a durned thing for nobody else!" Pete whined.

I cleared off the last of my potatoes and gravy and reached for the platter of chops. "I'll pay you for 'em."

Stunned silence.

"Also pay you for the full load of shelled corn I'll be needing."

"Why, Simon Green, you ain't got a plugged nickel to your name," Aunt Maybelle finally choked out.

Samson and Samantha were married but now they die, and Simon them son, now live withe his uncle Lucas.

stunned: in a state of disbelief

Reading: Ask clarifying questions (why, who, what)

"Don't now. Will by the end of summer."

"You expect me to let you have them mules and corn on speculation, Simon?" Uncle Lucas's piggy eyes spread as wide as they ever got.

I laid three more chops on my plate and dribbled the gravy nice and slow. "Yep. If you want to be rid of me for good and final."

The cousins started in nudging each other around me. Ned finally spoke up.

"Write out a contract, Pa. Make him sign it, nice and legal." Ned snickered. "He does know how to sign his name. Should, after four years in the third grade!" The snicker grew into a guffaw. Ned finally settled some. "Put down about how that there wagon is Simon's complete and full inheritance. And write down the price of the corn and mules, too. Going rates."

Aunt Maybelle got up from table. "How about some pie? In honor of our Simon's new business."

Nary a one of 'em asked me what that business might be.

Out in the backyard after supper, I stripped to my trousers and doused a bucket of water over my head and shoulders. Put on my clean Sunday shirt and slicked down my hair. Cousin Pete spied my efforts.

"Simon's got a sweetheart! Simon's got a sweetheart!"

I didn't deign to make an answer, just mounted my lead mule, Sparky, bareback, and took off down the road to Union. Sooner than later I got to the schoolhouse and knocked on the door back behind.

As You Read

1. Why does Cousin Pete say that Simon has a sweetheart?
2. What kind of work does Miss Rogers do?

deign: do something you feel is beneath your standing

Reading: Use context to find the meaning of unknown words

That's where Miss Rogers lived. She opened the door, a surprised look on her face.

"Why, Simon!"

"Evening, ma'am." I shuffled from one big foot to the other for a moment or two. All the time she kept on staring at me.

"You're all spruced up, Simon. What's the occasion?"

"Wondered if I might have a word, ma'am."

"That would be a rare pleasure. Even if we only parted this afternoon." She stood aside and waved me into her little room.

I hadn't ever been there before. Not in all these years of schooling. It was her private territory. Most creatures have one. Mine was beneath that same old wagon I'd just saved from rotting to death. Many's the summer's night I lay underneath its bed, just content to be away from the house and my cousins. Staring at the stars through the gaps in its slats, wondering if my mama was up there somewheres keeping an eye on me. Now I spun around slowly, taking in Miss Rogers's territory.

"I suspicioned it'd be nice. Like you."

She smiled. "Do take a seat, Simon. I'll fix us a cup of tea."

There were only two chairs by the tiny table in a corner. I took one of them. then I tried to figure on what to do with my long legs. They never seemed to get in the way like this in the schoolroom next door.

---

rare: uncommon

Reading: Use context to find the meaning of unknown words

A china cup was set in front of me. On a saucer. There was painted rosebuds all over both. The handle on that cup looked to break in pieces if I was to even touch it with my thick fingers. A matching teapot finally joined it all atop the lace tablecloth. Miss Rogers sat herself down across from me. She arranged her skirts.

"We'll just let the tea steep a moment, Simon."

"Yes, ma'am."

We waited, both staring at that teapot. Miss Rogers finally reached for it and poured for the both of us.

"There now." She smiled again. "You may begin, Simon. Tea does help to settle nerves, I've found."

I made a cup and managed not to disgrace myself. That tea was soothing. The cup skittered back into its saucer. I took a deep breath.

"It's about spreading my wings, ma'am. I've made a start on it."

One eyebrow rose. "Already?"

"Yes, ma'am. I've lined up the wagon and the mules and the corn. That leaves but the turkeys."

"Turkeys?" She set down her own cup. "Turkeys."

"Yes, ma'am. Mr. Buffey's got a thousand to spare, and I can have them for a quarter apiece . . ." Then I set my elbows on the table and started explaining. About Denver. And the turkey walk.

Miss Rogers listened all the way through. She really listened. By the time I got to the end, both

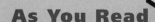

As You Read

1. Why does Miss Rogers offer Simon tea?

2. Where does Simon plan to take the wagon and the turkeys?

3. How does Simon want Miss Rogers to help him?

steep: soak to become flavorful

skittered: fell into place

Reading: Draw inferences or conclusions about text and support them with textual evidence

eyebrows had lifted clear up her forehead. She raised a hand and smoothed them back down again. "That is an amazing story, Simon."

"Ain't a story," I protested. "It's pure fact." I edged my elbows off the table. "And I know birds. I'm comfortable with them. It's something I can do, Miss Rogers!"

"Well." She remembered to pick up her cup again. "I do believe you could! How can I help?"

I knew exactly how she could help. That's why I'd come. "First off, my multiplication weren't ever too strong. But the numbers are nice and round. Wanted you to check them for me."

I pulled out a scrap of paper. "See here? One thousand turkeys times twenty-five cents." I glanced across to her. "Seems to me that'd make two hundred and fifty dollars."

Miss Rogers, she didn't even need to glance at my scrap. She just beamed. "You remembered about adding the zeros. And even moving the decimal point. I'm so proud of you, Simon!"

"Thank you, ma'am." That decimal point had given me a few bad moments. But now came the really hard part. I tried to figure on what to do with my hands, since they seemed to get in the way of conversing. I finally sat on them.

"That just leaves me with finding two hundred and fifty dollars to buy Mr. Buffey's flock. What I need is a partner, Miss Rogers. Come Denver, that partner's money would increase. Like loaves and fishes."

Miss Rogers's eyebrows, they rose some more. Sky-high.

Connecting to **Mathematics**

Simon plans to make a profit by selling the turkeys. He buys 1,000 turkeys at 25¢ per turkey. That means he pays $250.00 total.

scrap: a small piece

Reading: Draw inferences or conclusions about text and support them with textual evidence

Sparky and me, we trotted back home that night in clouds of glory. Miss Rogers had said it was the most interesting business proposition she'd ever heard. Especially coming from someone generally considered pea-brained. We had an appointment to meet at the town bank in the morning. Miss Rogers was going to invest her life savings from teaching in my turkey walk. Course, that meant I had to succeed. The saddest thing I could think of was having Miss Rogers lose her life savings.

Back at the farm, I unbridled Sparky and gave him a rub. Then I stroked the fine velvet on his long ears.

"You and me are going to have ourselves a time," I murmured to him. "You and me and your brothers. We're going to see the world. And we're going to make something of ourselves."

proposition: an idea or a plan

Reading: Ask clarifying questions (how, what)

After Sparky brayed his approval, I grabbed a saddle blanket and spread it under my wagon. Instead of counting the stars, I lay there figuring on how to fix it up strong. Really strong.

brayed: made a loud, harsh sound

About the Author

Kathleen Karr has written many books, some of which are historical fiction like *The Great Turkey Walk*. She grew up on a chicken farm in southern New Jersey, so she knows a lot about poultry. She lives in Washington, D.C. with her husband and two teenage children.

The Great Turkey Walk 43

After You Read

Retell it!

In a small group, take turns retelling the story out loud. Pay special attention to how the traits of the story's main characters affected what happened in the story.

Think, Discuss, Write

1. **Recall details** Who is Miss Rogers?

2. **Describe** What is Simon's problem? How does Simon think Miss Rogers can help the situation?

3. **Plot** What problems does Simon face in carrying out his plan? How does he go about solving these problems?

4. **Analyze** Make a list of Simon's character traits. How do these traits affect the events in the story? Which trait has the greatest effect on what happens in the story?

5. **Compare and contrast** Compare how different characters in the story, such as Miss Rogers and Simon's family members, treat Simon. Which characters seem to like and respect Simon more?

6. **Draw a conclusion** Why do you think Miss Rogers decided to give Simon her money? Which of her character traits helped her make the decision?

Writing: Write summaries that contain the main ideas of the reading

7. **Predict** How do you think "The Great Turkey Walk" will turn out? Will Simon earn money on his turkeys and return Miss Rogers' investment?

What's Your Opinion?

Simon describes himself as "pea-brained." Yet, there are many instances in the story where Simon seems to show that he is a pretty intelligent young man. Which is it: Is Simon smart or "pea-brained"? On a separate sheet of paper, make a list of reasons to support each side of the issue in a table like this one.

Simon is smart	Simon is pea-brained
Simon comes up with a clever plan	Simon is still in the third grade
Miss Rogers respects Simon	Simon's relatives don't seem to respect him

Launch into Grammar

Verb/compound subject agreement Some sentences contain more than one subject. When there are two or more nouns used as the subject, the verb must agree with its compound subject.

Example:

You and I are going to have ourselves a time.

With a partner, pick out four sentences in the reading with one subject. Rewrite each sentence in the present tense so there are two subjects and make sure that the verbs agree.

Written conventions: Identify and use subjects and verbs correctly

Launch into Word Analysis

Colloquial English   Sometimes writers use very informal, conversational language, colloquial language, to set a more realistic tone or to make a character more alive and colorful. Colloquial language contains words or phrases that certain areas of the country or certain cultures use in everyday speech.

   With a partner, reread the story and write down five sentences that contain colloquial English. Rewrite each sentence in a more formal, grammatically correct sentence. Which sentence is more interesting to you?

   Example:

   Informal: Got me graduated from school today. Fixing on setting up in business.

   Formal: I graduated from school today. I plan to open a business.

Launch into Writing

Use dialogue   Authors use **dialogue** to bring characters to life. Think about a recent situation that involved you and one other person. Write about that situation two times: once using dialogue, and the other time without dialogue. Which piece is more effective in conveying its message?

Reading: Understand and explain the figurative and metaphorical use of words in context

Here is an example:

At the Supper Table

During supper last night, I asked if I could have the old wagon behind the barn. Uncle Lucas said I could have it, because it was an inheritance from my mother, who was Uncle Lucas' sister Samantha.

At the Supper Table

"If I was to fix up that old wagon, could I have it?" I asked Uncle Lucas. "I'm fixing on setting up in business."

"Supposin' I was to give it to you," Uncle Lucas said. "Out of the kindness of my heart, as a sort of inheritance. In memory of my dear sister Samantha, departed these ten long years."

 For more practice writing dialogue, complete pages 30–31 of the Student Workbook.

Writing: Revise original drafts to provide more descriptive detail

Tell a Story

You have read several narratives in this unit. A narrative has a **beginning,** a **problem** or **conflict,** and an **ending** or **resolution.** This series of events is called the **plot.** The high point of the plot, or the most exciting part of the story, is the **climax.**

You will work in a small group and take turns telling stories. Choose a topic about a major change that happened in your life or to someone you know.

Step One: Plan Your Story

1. Discuss your story ideas. Decide on one that you would like to use. Select an idea that will interest your audience. Ask yourself:

   - What **kind of story** will be most interesting to my audience? Is it a scary story? A romantic story? Did the story really take place?

   - What **point of view** will be most appropriate? Am I describing something that happened to somebody else, or am I the hero of the story?

2. Make an outline: Include the beginning, the conflict or problem, the rising action that leads to the climax, and the ending or resolution.

3. Decide if you want to include some dialogue.

4. Decide who will tell each part of the story. You might want to divide the parts based on the beginning, conflict, rising action, climax, and ending.

Step Two: Practice Your Story

Practice telling each part of your story. Record your story and then listen to the recording. How can you improve your story? Use the Speaking Checklist on the next page to comment on another group's telling of their story.

Step Three: Tell Your Story

Once you have practiced telling your story, you are ready to tell it to the class. Have one member of your group be ready to answer questions that come up.

Writing: Create multiple-paragraph narrative compositions

Step Four: Evaluate Your Story

After telling your story, invite your audience to ask you questions or give you comments. Did your classmates enjoy your story? What suggestions do they have for improving your story or the way you told your story?

Record Your Story

Add a tape of your story to a classroom listening lab. Listen to your own and others' tapes. Check out a tape to share at home or with another class.

Speaking Checklist

✔ Use an appropriate tone of voice.

✔ Be sure to speak slowly enough to be clear. Do not speak so slowly that you lose your audience's attention. Pronounce your words clearly and correctly.

✔ Keep your body still.

✔ Make eye contact with the audience.

Reading: Read aloud with fluency in a manner that sounds like natural speech

Write a Personal Narrative

Recall an event from your childhood that changed you or made you think about something in a different way. Write a personal narrative about that experience. Use sensory details and concrete language to express your thoughts and feelings.

To write your personal narrative, follow the example below.

1. Pre-write

Think about your purpose and audience. Who will your readers be? What event changed your thinking? How should you tell about it? Decide what you are going to write about. Jot down memories, including details about the people, place, and event.

> ### Harold, Kiki, and Duke
>
> Ever since last year, I began to call myself "lucky." When I was seven, my cousin gave me two German Shepherd puppies. I named them Harold and Kiki. They liked to relax, play ball, and swim in the lake.
>
> Then, last year, someone left the gate open and Harold and Kiki got away. I was very upset. My parents got me a new dog. I named him Duke. I still missed Harold and Kiki a lot, but it was nice to play with Duke.
>
> You may wonder why I call myself "lucky." My other dogs were found and brought back home. Now I have three dogs to play with.

Writing: Write descriptions of a real event, using sensory details

2. Draft

Follow these steps to organize your personal narrative.

A. Include the time and place. Be sure the setting is clear.

B. Write in your own voice, using "I," "me," and "my." Use sensory details and concrete language to help your readers share your memory.

C. Tell how the experience changed you. At the end of your narrative, tell what you learned.

Refer to the notes you jotted down to guide you as you draft your personal narrative.

3. Revise

Reread your draft and ask yourself these questions:

- Have I included the time and place?
- Have I told the events in the order they occurred?
- Have I used sensory details and concrete language?
- Have I told the reader how the experience changed me?

Ask a classmate to answer these same questions about your narrative.

Make any additional changes based on your classmate's feedback.

4. Edit and Proofread

Proofread your revised narrative. Check sentence punctuation, capitalization, and spelling. Look in the dictionary to verify spellings.

5. Publish

Make your personal narrative into a book. Follow these steps:

A. Create a title for your narrative.

B. Decide which part of the narrative should be on each page.

C. Recopy or retype the text for each page and glue it onto poster board.

D. Add illustrations to your book.

E. Share your book with the class.

Writing: Revise drafts, to improve coherence and progression

Story Sequels

Project Goal

In this unit you read about the different changes people experience every day. For this project you will create written sequels. Sequels are a continuation of a story. Your sequel will be a short story (four to five paragraphs) that continues the story from one of the chapters. You will write about one of the characters and what he or she has learned from a change.

1. Choose which story and character you are going to write about. Decide what change the character might experience next. Before you start to write, make a list and answer the following:

- What type of change does the character experience?
- What causes this change?
- How does he or she deal with this change?
- Do others help him or her with this change?

- How does he or she finally feel about this change?
- What does he or she learn from this change?

Example: At the end of "Dia's Story Cloth," Dia returns to Laos to help refugee women. What might happen to her next? Perhaps Dia meets a woman from her village who knows what happened to her father, and that he is still alive.

Example: At the end of the excerpt from "The Great Turkey Walk," Simon is preparing to go to Denver to sell his turkeys. What might happen to him there? Will he meet with success? Could something go wrong with his plan?

2. After answering the questions, start to write your short story. Ask a partner to read your story and give you feedback.

Words to Know

sequels	continuation
change	learn
journey	

Writing: Write narratives—establish plot and develop character, using a range of narrative devices

Choose one or more of the following books to read. Write in your Reading Log the books you read and your opinion of each. Ask yourself these questions:

1. What is the plot of the story?
2. Is this story fiction or nonfiction?
3. How did this book address the theme of changes?
4. Did you like this book? Why or why not?

Nonfiction

Discovering El Niño: How Fable and Fact Together Help Explain the Weather by Patricia Seibert
   The author shows how basic scientific thinking is used to predict changes in the weather.

Diary of a Young Girl by Anne Frank
   This diary of a young Jewish girl who lived in Hitler's Germany has become a beloved classic since it was first published in 1947.

Fiction

Janey's Girl by Gayle Friesen
   In this nominee for Young Reader's Choice Award, Claire and her mother pay a visit to Claire's grandmother. Claire decides to learn the mystery of her own and her mother's past.

Bud, Not Buddy by Christopher Paul Curtis
   In this Newbery Medal Book set in the 1930s, Bud "not Buddy" Caldwell is a ten-year-old orphan who leaves his foster homes behind in search of his father.

Reading: Compare and contrast information on the same topic

UNIT 2
Heroes

"Leadership and learning are indispensable to each other."

— John F. Kennedy (U.S. president, 1917–1963)

Discuss the Theme
Becoming a Hero

There are many ways to be a hero. In this unit, you will read
about a father whose imagination and ability to create an
entire fictional world make him a hero in his son's eyes. You
will read about two mothers whose quiet strength makes them
heroes to their daughters. You will also learn how millions of
people just like us heroically give up their time, money, and
energy to help others. And finally, you will find out about a
woman who has spent her entire adult life working with
chimpanzees in Africa.

- What words describe a hero? What kinds of things do
  heroes do?
- Who are your heroes? Why do you admire them?
- Do you think you are a hero to anyone?
- Do you know somebody who has taken risks to help
  people in trouble?

WRITING FOCUS:
Expository Essay

Background

Can a person be a hero just by telling stories? What kinds of stories do you like to listen to and read? In the short story you are going to read, a father creates a fictional character who is larger than life, in more ways than one.

LEARNING OBJECTIVES

- Identify and analyze themes created by characters, actions, and images
- Identify and interpret figurative language
- Use indefinite pronouns
- Write a review that includes a thesis statement

The Big Friendly Giant

a story by Roald Dahl

Building Your Vocabulary

1. In this story, a father tells his son a bedtime story that goes on and on. With a partner, sort the phrases by creating a chart like the one at the top of page 57. If they go with the real-life world of the father and son, put them under **Real Life.** If they go with the made-up world of "The Big Friendly Giant," put them under **Fictional World.**

Reading: Make predictions about text by using prior knowledge, titles, and important words

father and his son

vast underground cavern _no_

magic powder

hands as big as wheelbarrows

in front of the wood stove _no_

Big Friendly Giant _no_

bedtime story _yes_

my father kissed me

Real Life	Fictional World
father and his son	*Big Friendly Giant*

2. After you read the story, come back and check your work.

Reading Strategy

Identify themes communicated through characters, actions, and images Writers communicate the theme, or central message, of a reading in many ways. Images give clues to the author's message. The descriptions of characters and their actions also tell you what the author is trying to say.

Applying the Reading Strategy

1. Pay attention to the images that the author presents. Do you see a pattern of images? One reading may present bright cheerful images while the images of a second reading might be dark and gloomy. Each pattern helps the author establish a central message, or theme.

2. Pay attention to how characters are described and the characters' actions.

Keep in mind that actions often speak louder than words. Both descriptions and actions can help you understand a reading's theme.

3. Take notes under three headings: Images, Character Descriptions, and Actions. Look at your notes after you finish reading and use them to understand the reading's theme.

Reading: Discern main ideas in texts, identify evidence that supports these ideas

The Big Friendly Giant

a story by Roald Dahl

My father, without the slightest doubt, was the most marvelous and exciting father any boy ever had. Here is a picture of him.

You might think, if you didn't know him well, that he was a stern and serious man. He wasn't. He was actually a wildly funny person. What made him appear so serious was the fact that he never smiled with his mouth. He did it all with his eyes. He had brilliant blue eyes and when he thought of something funny, his eyes would flash and, if you looked carefully, you could actually see a tiny little golden spark dancing in the middle of each eye. But the mouth never moved.

I was glad my father was an eye-smiler. It meant he never gave me a fake smile because it's impossible to make your eyes twinkle if you aren't feeling twinkly yourself. A mouth-smile is different. You can fake a mouth-smile any time you want, simply by moving your lips. I've also learned that a real mouth-smile always has an eye-smile to go with it. So watch out, I say, when someone smiles at you with his mouth but his eyes stay the same. It's sure to be a phony.

My father was not what you would call an educated man. I doubt he had read twenty books in his life. But he was a marvelous storyteller. He used to make up a bedtime story for me every single night, and the best

As You Read

1. What is the father like? What two words does the narrator use to describe him?

2. What kind of storyteller is the father?

3. What is the main character in the father's story like?

Reading: Discern main ideas in texts

ones were turned into serials and went on for many nights running.

One of them, which must have gone on for at least fifty nights, was about an enormous fellow called "The Big Friendly Giant," or "The BFG" for short. The BFG was three times as tall as an ordinary man and his hands were as big as wheelbarrows. He lived in a vast underground cavern not far from our filling station and he only came out into the open when it was dark. Inside the cavern he had a powder factory where he made more than one hundred different kinds of magic powder.

Occasionally, as he told his stories, my father would stride up and down waving his arms and waggling his fingers. But most times

Building Your Vocabulary

As you read, list unfamiliar words in your Vocabulary Log.

serials: stories that appear regularly in a series of parts
filling station: British word for gas station

Reading: Discern main ideas in texts

he would sit close to me on the edge of my bunk and speak very softly.

"The Big Friendly Giant makes his magic powders out of the dreams that children dream when they are asleep," he said.

"How?" I asked. "Tell me how, dad."

"Dreams, my love, are very mysterious things. They float around in the night air like little clouds, searching for sleeping people."

"Can you see them?" I asked.

"Nobody can see them."

"Then how does The Big Friendly Giant catch them?"

"Ah," my father said, "that is the interesting part. A dream, you see, as it goes drifting through the night air, makes a tiny little buzzing-humming sound, a sound so soft and low it is impossible for ordinary people to hear it. But The BFG can hear it easily. His sense of hearing is absolutely fantastic."

I loved the intent look on my father's face when he was telling a story. His face was pale and still and distant, unconscious of everything around him.

"The BFG," he said, "can hear the tread of a ladybug's footsteps as she walks across a leaf. He can hear the whisperings of ants as they scurry around in the soil talking to one another. He can hear the sudden shrill cry of pain a tree gives out when a woodman cuts into it with an ax.

tread: footstep
scurry: to move quickly

As You Read

1. What are some of the things The BFG can hear?

Ah yes, my darling, there is a whole world of sound around us that we cannot hear because our ears are simply not sensitive enough."

"What happens when he catches the dreams?" I asked.

"He imprisons them in glass bottles and screws the tops down tight," my father said. "He has thousands of these bottles in his cave."

"Does he catch bad dreams as well as good ones?"

"Yes," my father said. "He catches both. But he only uses the good ones in his powders."

"What does he do with the bad ones?"

"He explodes them."

It is impossible to tell you how much I loved my father. When he was sitting close to me on my bunk I would reach out and slide my hand into his, and then he would fold his long fingers around my fist, holding it tight.

"What does The BFG do with his powders after he has made them?" I asked.

"In the dead of night," my father said, "he goes prowling through the villages searching for houses where children are asleep. Because of his great height he can reach windows that are two and even three flights up, and when he finds a room with a sleeping child, he opens his suitcase—"

"His suitcase?" I said.

As You Read

1. How does The BFG catch dreams?

2. What does The BFG do with the dreams he catches? What does he do with the bad dreams?

3. Does the narrator love his father? How can you tell?

"The BFG always carries a suitcase and a blowpipe," my father said. "The blowpipe is as long as a lamppost. The suitcase is for the powders. So he opens the suitcase and selects exactly the right powder—and he puts it into the blowpipe—and he slides the blowpipe in through the open window—and poof!—he blows in the powder—and the powder floats around the room—and the child breathes it in—"

"And then what?" I asked.

"And then, Danny, the child begins to dream a marvelous and fantastic dream—and when the dream reaches its most marvelous and fantastic moment—then the magic powder really takes over—and suddenly the dream is not a dream any longer but a real happening—and the child is not asleep in bed—he is fully awake and is actually in the place of the dream and is taking part in the whole thing—I mean really taking part—in real life. More about that tomorrow. It's getting late. Good night, Danny. Go to sleep."

My father kissed me and then he turned down the wick of the little kerosene lamp until the flame went out. He seated himself in front of the wood stove which now made a lovely red glow in the dark room.

"Dad," I whispered.

"What is it?"

"Have you ever actually seen The Big Friendly Giant?"

"Once," my father said. "Only once."

"You did! Where?"

As You Read

1. Has the father ever seen The BFG?
2. Was the father afraid when he saw The BFG?
3. What does he say about his experience?

Reading: Discern main ideas in texts

"I was out behind the caravan," my father said, "and it was a clear moonlit night, and I happened to look up and suddenly I saw this tremendous tall person running along the crest of the hill. He had a queer long-striding lolloping gait and his black cloak was streaming out behind him like the wings of a bird. There was a big suitcase in one hand and a blowpipe in the other, and when he came to the high hawthorne hedge at the end of the field, he just strode over it as though it wasn't there."

"Were you frightened, Dad?"

"No," my father said. "It was thrilling to see him, and a little eerie, but I wasn't frightened. Go to sleep now. Good night."

caravan: British word for trailer

gait: way of walking

hawthorne hedge: a row of small, thorny trees

About the Author

Roald Dahl

Roald Dahl is considered one of the best storytellers of our time. Some of his most popular books, *James and the Giant Peach, Charlie and the Chocolate Factory,* and *Matilda,* are widely read the world over and have even been made into movies. Roald Dahl was born in Wales to Norwegian parents.

Reading: Discern main ideas in texts

After You Read

Retell It!

Work in small groups. Use the notes you took when you read "The Big Friendly Giant." Take turns retelling the story out loud.

Think, Discuss, Write

In your group, discuss and write your answers. What do the two stories have in common?

1. **Plot** How many times did the father see The Big Friendly Giant?

2. **Plot** What did the father do for his son every night?

3. **Plot** What did The Big Friendly Giant do for the town's children?

4. **Characterization** What kind of person is Danny's father?

5. **Characterization** What kind of person is The Big Friendly Giant?

6. **Characterization** What did Danny's father and The Big Friendly Giant have in common?

7. **Recurrent theme** Who are the heroes of the story?

Reading: Make reasonable assertions through accurate, supporting citations

What's Your Opinion?

Is there someone in your life who is a good storyteller like Danny's father? What characteristics are necessary to be a good storyteller? Make a list of the characteristics of a good storyteller. You can use the characteristics listed below and any others you think are important. List the characteristics in order of importance.

- a good speaking voice
- good ideas for stories
- a sense of humor
- a good imagination

Launch into Grammar

Indefinite pronouns A **pronoun** is a word that replaces a **noun**. (Nouns are words that stand for people, places, and things.) Pronouns include such words as *I, you, he, she, they,* and *it.* Some pronouns stand for a specific noun:

Example: *Arthur* fell down. → *He* fell down.

Here, the pronoun *he* replaces *Arthur.* Other pronouns are **indefinite**. Indefinite pronouns don't stand for any noun in particular:

Example: *Someone* fell down.

The person who fell isn't identified. Indefinite pronouns include: *anyone, everyone, anybody, somebody, no one,* and *nothing.* Use one of the indefinite pronouns listed to complete each sentence on page 66. Work with a partner.

Written conventions: Identify and properly use indefinite pronouns

nothing   some   someone

1. I'm looking for _____ who likes stories.

2. There is _____ better than a good story.

3. _____ stories are better than others.

 For more practice with indefinite pronouns, use page 26 of the Student Workbook.

Extend: Find three song titles that have indefinite pronouns, such as *Don't You Want Somebody to Love?* Share your song titles with the class.

Launch into Word Analysis

Hyperbole   Writers sometimes stretch the truth in order to make a point. For example, to say you like your father is one thing. To say that your father is "the most marvelous and exciting father any boy ever had" is an example of **hyperbole**, or exaggeration.

The author of "The Big Friendly Giant" uses hyperbole for several reasons. Hyperbole gets your point across—there is no mistaking the boy's feelings for his father. Hyperbole is also colorful, vivid, and can be quite funny in some situations.

With a partner, find three examples of hyperbole in the story. Then write three sentences of your own that use hyperbole.

 For more practice with hyperbole, use page 36 of the Student Workbook.

Reading: Identify and interpret figurative language

Launch into Writing

Create a thesis statement   Writers use a **thesis statement** when they want to be very clear about a point. A thesis statement directly tells the point an author wants to make about a subject, for example: *"The Big Friendly Giant" is the best story Roald Dahl ever wrote.*

A thesis statement often comes at the beginning of a paragraph. It should be written in clear, direct language, so there is no mistake about the meaning. Here are some other examples of thesis statements.

> *In this section, I will explain why I think Roald Dahl was a great writer.*
>
> *There was no doubt that childhood was an important time for Dahl.*
>
> *The Twits was perhaps Dahl's funniest book.*

Write a short review of "The Big Friendly Giant." Be sure to include a thesis statement in your review. Back up your thesis statement using facts, examples, and arguments that support your point.

 For more practice with thesis statements, use pages 38–39 of the Student Workbook.

Writing: Write expository compositions: state the thesis, explain the situation, offer evidence to validate arguments

6

Hope

a poem by
Janet S. Wong

When
Tonya's Friends
Come to
Spend the Night

a poem by
Eloise Greenfield

Before You Read

Background

Who are the people in your family you admire? Why do you admire them? In the two poems you are going to read, you will learn about two mothers. You will find out why their daughters admire them.

Building Your Vocabulary

1. You are going to read two poems about mothers. In the first one, the poet compares mothers to things in nature. The second poem describes how loving a mother is even to her daughter's friends. Look at the following phrases and write them in the correct area in a chart like the one on page 69.

   - the strength of a bear
   - tells them that she loves them
   - feeds them sweet banana bread
   - the softness of a deer
   - the calm of a tree
   - hugs them when it's time for bed
   - listens to what they can do
   - the courage of a fox

Reading: Interpret information from diagrams and charts

Qualities of Nature Mothers Have	Ways Mothers Show Love

2. Compare your chart with a partner's. Discuss any differences. Based on your answers, which poem do you want to read more?

Reading Strategy

Identify and analyze themes by looking at symbols and metaphors Writers use **symbols** to stand for things. A symbol is an object or image that suggests, or stands for, something else. Most people understand that a dove is a symbol of peace. A sunrise is a symbol of hope. A king's crown is a symbol of power. Symbols like these can communicate the themes, or central messages, of a poem.

Applying the Reading Strategy

1. As you read, look for striking images that catch your eye. The author could be using these vivid images as symbols to suggest, or stand for, some important thought or idea in the poem. Make a note of each image or thing.

2. As you read the poem, look for the themes, or central messages, that the author is trying to communicate. Make a note of each theme.

3. Try to link the images that you noted with the important themes in the poem. If an image really works as a symbol, it should increase your understanding and enjoyment of the poem.

4. Be flexible in the way that you interpret symbols. Keep in mind that symbols do not have to be complete or absolute. A sunset, for example, could symbolize the "end" of something. But it could also stand for the beginning of something else!

Reading: Draw inferences about text and support them with textual evidence and prior knowledge

Hope

a poem by Janet S. Wong

In my own mother

I can see

I will need the strength of a bear,
strength to threaten those who would hurt my child—

Give me this strength.
I will need the softness of a deer,
to nudge my child down the right path—

Give me this softness.

I will need the courage of a fox
to leave my child behind, drawing harm my way—

Give me this courage.

I will need the calm of a tree,
knowing fires will happen,

and I will need to keep the hope I hold inside myself,
knowing that after the fires,

things grow again.

nudge: push gently.

As You Read

1. What will the strength of the bear help the mother do?
2. What will the softness of a deer help the mother do?
3. What will the courage of a fox help the mother do?
4. What will the calm of a tree help the mother do?

About the Author

Janet S. Wong

Janet S. Wong is a person of Chinese and Korean heritage. She was born in the United States. She uses a variety of styles in her poetry, including free verse, rhymed verse, haiku, and **cinquains** (stanzas with five lines). The poems in *The Rainbow Hand*, which include "Hope," were inspired by her memories of her mother and her own experiences as a mother to her son.

Reading: Draw inferences about text

When Tonya's Friends Come to Spend the Night

a poem by Eloise Greenfield

When Tonya's friends come to spend the night
Her mama's more than just polite
She says she's glad they came to call
Tells them that she loves them all
Listens to what they can do
Tells them what she's good at, too
Plays her horn and lets them sing
(Do they make that music swing!)
Feeds them sweet banana bread
Hugs them when it's time for bed
Tonya sure would have a gripe
If she were the jealous type
But she isn't just a guest
She knows her mama loves her best

As You Read

1. How does Tonya's mother treat her friends?

2. What do Tonya's friends tell her mother?

3. What does her mother tell her friends?

About the Author

Eloise Greenfield

Eloise Greenfield often works with the illustrator Jan Spivey Gilchrist, and together they have won both the Coretta Scott King Honor Award and the Coretta Scott King Medal. The poem *When Tonya's Friends Come to Spend the Night* comes from their book *Night on Neighborhood Street*.

After You Read

Retell It!

In small groups, memorize and recite the poems for your class. Make each member of your group responsible for memorizing and reciting one small section of each poem. Then use your own words to tell what each poem is mainly about.

Think, Discuss, Write

In your group, discuss and write answers to these questions.

1. **Recall details**   What does Janet S. Wong need to be like her mother?

2. **Recall details**   What instrument does Tonya's mother play for her friends?

3. **Compare and contrast**   Which poem is based on ideas or thoughts? What are they?

4. **Recurring themes**   Do the poems appeal to your senses (sight, smell, sound, taste, and touch)? How do they do this?

5. **Recurring themes**   What is the main theme or central message of both of these poems?

6. **Compare and contrast**   How are these poems similar or different?

7. **Compare and contrast**   Which poem has clearly described characters? Which poem has ideas, rather than characters?

Reading: Compare and contrast information on the same topic

What's Your Opinion?

Work in small groups. On a separate sheet of paper complete a diagram with words from the poems. Follow the example. Then discuss with your group members. Which poem did you like better? Why?

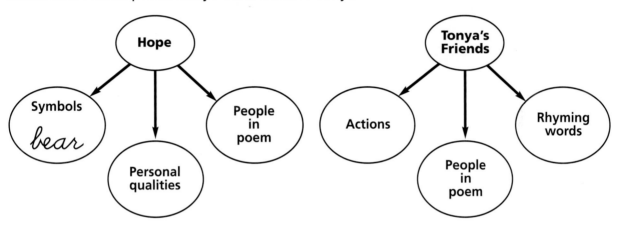

Launch into Grammar

Possessives Words that show ownership are called **possessives**. There are three main ways to show ownership.

- Use an **apostrophe** and an **s**: *Tonya's house, mama's horn.* For plurals that end in **s**, put the apostrophe at the end of the word: *the girl**s'** music, the friend**s'** pizza*

- Use **possessive adjectives** with **nouns**: *my friends, **your** house, **her** mother*

- Use **possessive pronouns** without **nouns**: *mine, yours, its, theirs*

- Use the word *of* with a **noun**: *the strength of a bull*

Hope *and* When Tonya's Friends Come to Spend the Night   73

Find as many examples of possessives as you can in the poems "Hope" and "When Tonya's Friends Come to Spend the Night." Put them into one of the four categories: **Apostrophe-s, Possessive adjectives with nouns, Possessive pronouns without nouns,** and **Of with nouns**.

 For more practice with possessive adjectives, apostrophes, and the word **of**, use page 43 of the Student Workbook.

Extend: Find a movie title or television program that includes each type of possessive.

Launch into Word Analysis

Contractions A **contraction** combines two words into one shorter word using an apostrophe.

Example: you + would → you'd
she + will   → she'll
can + not   → can't

The apostrophe takes the place of the letters that are missing in the contraction. The words *he* and *will* combine to form *he'll*. The apostrophe takes the place of the missing letters *wi*.

With a partner, find the contractions in "When Tonya's Friends Come to Spend the Night." Put each contraction into a table like the one below.

 For more practice with contractions, use page 44 of the Student Workbook.

First Word	Second Word	Contraction
she	*is*	*she's*

Written conventions: Identify and correctly use various parts of speech

Launch into Writing

Structure paragraphs Paragraphs can be structured in a variety of ways. The most common paragraph structure begins with a topic sentence that tells what your subject is. Follow the topic sentence with supporting sentences that provide facts, examples, and information to support the topic sentence. Finally, end the paragraph with a sentence that ties up loose ends and brings the topic to a close.

Practice structuring paragraphs by writing a paragraph about a mother that you know. Be sure that your paragraph: (1) begins with a topic sentence, (2) includes supporting sentences, and (3) ends with a closing sentence. Here is an example:

> My older sister Tamara is one of the best mothers I know. Only a few years ago, she was just my sister. Then, two years ago she had a baby. She does everything for that baby. I hope I'll be as patient as Tamara if I ever have a baby.

 For more practice with structuring paragraphs, use pages 46–47 of the Student Workbook.

Writing: Create a single paragraph: Develop a topic sentence, include supporting details

7

Before You Read

Background

What are the qualities of a hero? Do you know any heroes? What makes people heroes? In this chapter's reading, an excerpt from the nonfiction book *Who Cares? Millions Do . . .* you learn some things about heroes that may surprise you.

Who Cares?
Millions Do...

an excerpt from a nonfiction book by Milton Meltzer

LEARNING OBJECTIVES

- Look at text that uses a compare-and-contrast organization
- Identify and use comparatives
- Use the present perfect tense
- Write a comparative essay

Building Your Vocabulary

This selection comes from a book about **altruism,** or the ability to put others' needs ahead of your own. Altruism is the opposite of **an uncaring attitude.**

1. With a partner, put the words and phrases at the top of page 77 into the correct position in a chart like the one shown.

2. As you read the selection, write down words related to altruism and an uncaring attitude in your chart.

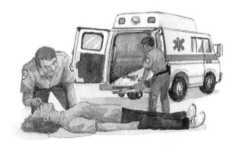

Reading: Use knowledge of antonyms to determine meanings of words

For words that you do not know, use a dictionary
to find their meanings.

unfeeling   hero   volunteer   helping   slavery
compassion   social action   oppression   discrimination   concern for others

Altruism	An Uncaring Attitude
hero	*unfeeling*

Reading Strategy

Compare-and-contrast organization   In writing,
many stories and articles are organized using a
structure that compares one thing to another. First
one thing is described, then the other. Similarities
show up. Differences stand out. By noticing this side-
by-side structure, you get a very clear idea of each
item being compared.

Applying the Reading Strategy

1. As you read, look for a compare-and-
   contrast structure. First, the author will
   introduce and define both things being
   compared in a general way.

2. Next, the author will get more specific.
   Facts and details about one of the two
   things will be listed. The first set of facts
   and details will be followed by a second
   set that describes the second thing being
   compared. Similarities and differences

   will be pointed out. Look for key words
   such as: *same, different, similar, alike,
   unlike, more, better,* or *on the other hand.*

3. As a careful reader, your job is to keep
   track of similarities and differences,
   strengths and weaknesses, and
   advantages and disadvantages of the two
   things being compared. Try taking notes
   as you read.

Reading: Analyze text that uses the compare-and-contrast organizational pattern

Who Cares? Millions Do...

an excerpt from a nonfiction book by Milton Meltzer

History

This reading includes references to examples of **oppression.** Oppression occurs when one group **discriminates** against another. Usually this takes place because the two groups are of different races, religions, or political backgrounds. Historic examples of oppression include Europeans taking land from Native Americans, making Africans slaves, and the laws against the Jews which were passed by the Nazis in Germany.

This is a book about that other side of American life.

Altruism, it's called.

It means a concern for and devotion to the interests of others. It's commonly used as the opposite of egoism, or selfishness.

A word confined to the dictionary, sniff the cynics. But in real life, here and now? What place does altruism have? Who cares about anyone but "me"?

Lots of people do. More than 105 million Americans volunteer an average of four hours a week to help causes or individuals. Of this number, 98 million are adults, and nearly 8 million are fourteen-to seventeen-year-olds. The value of their volunteer time is estimated at $174 billion a year. But you can't put a dollar sign on their worth; it's priceless.

Perhaps the most dramatic examples of unselfish behavior are heroes or heroines. They are the people we honor because of their exceptional service to humankind. They help others when there is no possible gain for themselves. In fact, their courageous deeds often place their own lives in jeopardy.

We've read about great heroes of the past in world literature, in the romances and epics of many cultures. Everyone knows about the Congressional Medal of Honor awarded for extraordinary heroism

cynics: people who believe that self-interest is the only motive for actions

romances: stories about love

epics: stories about heroic actions

Reading: Analyze text that uses the compare-and–contrast organizational pattern

in wartime. But there are men, women, and children in time of peace who also act to rescue their fellows. Here are just two of them:

- Jerry L. Conrad, thirty-five, of Toledo, Ohio, who leaped into a moving car to save a three-year-old girl.
- Allen N. Davidson, thirteen, of Gaffney, South Carolina, who crawled into a burning house and dragged an elderly woman to safety.

These examples of heroism are taken from the lists of people honored each year by the Carnegie Hero Fund. It recognizes outstanding acts of selfless heroism performed in the United States and Canada. Established in 1904, it has honored nearly 7,500 North Americans since that time.

We know of course that even heroes are not perfect. It's almost certain that none of those awarded Carnegie Medals were without weakness or blemish. Heroes are often "ordinary people who somehow manage to do extraordinary things," as the writer Madeline L'Engle has pointed out. "The heroic personality is human, not perfect, but human. And to be human is to be fallible." If you trace heroes through literature and legend and history, you see how often heroes make terrible mistakes. What matters is their ability to stretch themselves beyond their limitations at times of crisis.

A Carnegie Medal.

blemish: a flaw
fallible: able to make mistakes

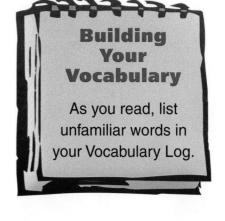

Building Your Vocabulary

As you read, list unfamiliar words in your Vocabulary Log.

As You Read

1. According to the author, are there many people who care or only a few people who care?

2. What is the worth in dollars of the total amount of time donated by volunteers in the U.S. each year?

3. The author gives two examples of heroes. Are these people famous people or ordinary people like us?

Reading: Analyze text that uses the compare-and–contrast organizational pattern

Mother Teresa.

This gives the rest of us hope. Maybe we can do it, too. The seed of altruism is within ourselves, wanting to spring forth and grow.

There is more than one kind of heroism. What the Carnegie Medal singles out are the emergencies that involve threat of harm or actual harm, and the selfless heroism of people who come to the rescue.

What about the people who express their altruism in social action, and do it daily? They are able to identify with others—in need, in trouble, in danger—to do what many of us are afraid to do, fearing the threats and sacrifices that come with commitment to others.

Mother Teresa is an example recognized and admired the world over. The Yugoslavian nun worked more than forty years among the desperately poor of Calcutta, India. She founded the Roman Catholic Missionaries of Charity who live no better than the poor among whom they work in dozens of countries. Mother Teresa and her coworkers did not try to convert others. They simply tended "the poorest of the poor," to live out, as she said, "that life of love, of compassion, that God has for his people." To her the rights of others not only mattered as much as her own but mattered even more, in a true spirit of selflessness.

The same spirit emerges from the pages of our pre–Civil War history. We read of abolitionists who devoted their lives to the struggle to end slavery. Some of them, at great risk, went into the South to rescue black people from bondage. Perhaps 2,000 slaves a year escaped from their masters,

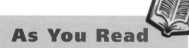

As You Read

1. Who was Mother Teresa?
2. What did the abolitionists do?

Reading: Analyze text that uses the compare-and–contrast organizational pattern

most of them through their own ingenuity and daring. Many fugitive slaves, however, were helped to freedom by African-Americans or by whites. Harriet Tubman, born into slavery in Maryland, ran away to freedom at the age of twenty-nine. Working as a domestic in Pennsylvania, she managed to save enough money to finance periodic trips to the South to rescue family and friends. She made nineteen of these dangerous trips, freeing, she estimated, more than 300 slaves. During the Civil War, in her early forties, she served in South Carolina for three years as a spy, scout, and nurse for the Union army. She lived into her nineties.

One of the white "conductors" on the Underground Railroad was Calvin Fairbank. Born in upstate New York in the early 1800s, he became a circuit preacher on the frontier while still a youngster. Gradually he moved toward abolitionism. One day he decided to do more than preach against slavery among Northerners. He would identify himself with the black people "that are in bonds as bound with them." So he crossed the Ohio River into Kentucky. It was in this slave state that most of his daring rescues took place. He helped dozens of slaves reach free soil. He was caught twice and sentenced to prison each time, serving a total of seventeen years behind bars.

More than a hundred years later another group of Americans, black and white, like Tubman and Fairbank, went into the South again. This time

Harriet Tubman.

As You Read

1. Who was Harriet Tubman? What did she do that makes her a hero?

2. Who was Calvin Fairbank? What did he do to become a hero?

3. How is the work that Calvin Fairbank did different from what Harriet Tubman did? How is it similar?

ingenuity: cleverness

domestic: a household servant

Reading: Analyze text that uses the compare-and–contrast organizational pattern

African-American soldiers in World War II.

their mission was to register African-Americans to vote. Using local ordinances, threat of job loss, and violence, white racists had succeeded in preventing most blacks from exercising their right to register and vote. For though the Civil War had ended slavery, it did not end discrimination and segregation. Black people still lived in poverty and were oppressed. They seemed free in name only. Jim Crow laws narrowly restricted their lives. Even their participation in the U. S. armed forces that helped win victory over Hitler's Nazi system in World War II did not change many things for African-Americans.

Then in 1954 the Supreme Court's Brown v. Board of Education decision revolutionized American education. The court declared that separate schools for blacks and whites were unconstitutional, and called for an end to segregation. When the legal barriers fell in education, a dream was rekindled in the heart of black America—to live in a nation where all people were treated equally and were not judged by the color of their skin. In the 1950s blacks began the modern civil rights movement to make that dream become a reality. Activists used boycotts, sit-ins, freedom rides, picketing, and mass marches to advance the cause.

One of the organizations founded to speed victory was the Student Nonviolent Coordinating Committee (SNCC). Its objective was to promote integration in the South. In 1964 SNCC conducted the Mississippi Summer Project, hoping to bring about changes in that most backward of states through black voter registration and education. SNCC volunteers

boycotts: joining with others in refusing to use a certain product or service

Reading: Analyze text that uses the compare-and–contrast organizational pattern

included about 1,000 northern students, lawyers, doctors, ministers, and teachers, from all over the country. About half were young whites, many of them of upper-middle-class background. They underwent intensive training on an Ohio campus and then went down to Mississippi to begin their work.

They organized fifty freedom schools and established another fifty community centers.

That summer in Mississippi the unprovoked killing of African-Americans multiplied and went unpunished. There were over 1,000 arrests of the young freedom volunteers. Thirty were wounded by gunfire, and three young organizers—James Chaney, Andrew Goodman, and Michael Schwerner—were murdered by white terrorists.

What made these young men and women volunteer in the face of such dangers? Religious values? Secular values? A spirit of adventure? "All of these," suggests the Harvard psychiatrist and author Robert Coles, who interviewed many of them, "and maybe any number of idiosyncratic motives."

Freedom marchers in Washington, D.C.

As You Read

1. What is the SNCC?
2. Who were James Chaney, Andrew Goodman, and Michael Schwerner?

idiosyncratic: something specific to one person's way of thinking

About the Author

Milton Meltzer

Milton Meltzer has written almost ninety books and has won many awards. Some of his most recent books, besides *Who Cares? Millions Do...*, are *Cheap Raw Material, Gold, Lincoln in His Own Words,* and *The Amazing Potato.* He and his wife live in New York City.

Reading: Analyze text that uses the compare-and-contrast organizational pattern

After You Read

Retell It!

Work in pairs. Choose one of the heroes from the reading and have a conversation with a partner. Compare the histories of the heroes you choose.

Think, Discuss, Write

In pairs, discuss the answers to these questions. Then write them down.

1. **Recall details**   About how many fourteen- to seventeen-year-olds volunteer their time to help others?

2. **Recall details**   What Supreme Court decision revolutionized American education?

3. **Recall details**   What are the names of some of the heroes mentioned in the story?

4. **Connect recurring themes**   What personality traits do certain heroes have in common?

5. **Describe**   What are the different types of heroism?

6. **Connect recurring themes**   Do you think that it is important for people to believe in altruism?

7. **Explain**   How does altruism help our society and our world?

What's Your Opinion?

Work with a partner. Each person should choose a favorite story from the heroes mentioned in the excerpt. Together, fill out a chart like the one on page 85 to show your opinions.

Reading: Use knowledge of the author's purpose to comprehend informational text

Favorite hero	Kind of hero	Reason why this hero is your favorite
Calvin Fairbank	*abolitionist*	*Helped dozens of slaves*

Launch into Grammar

The present perfect tense The **present perfect tense** uses the verb *have* in the present tense with a second verb that has a past participle ending, often *ed*. Don't be fooled by the word *present*. The present perfect is used to refer to the past.

Example: She *has helped* at the soup kitchen.

Use the present perfect tense when you don't want to be specific about the past. Compare the past and present perfect tenses.

Example: Past: I *cleaned* the car this morning.
Present perfect: I *have cleaned* the car.

The past tense tells you exactly when something happened. The present perfect tense lets you be less specific about when something occurred. Work with a partner. On a separate piece of paper, write sentences using the present perfect tense of the verb in parentheses.

1. Jerry L. Conrad (save) a girl from danger.

2. Allen N. Davidson (crawl) into a burning house to save a woman.

Written conventions: Identify and use verb tenses in the past

For more practice with the present perfect tense, use page 51 of the Student Workbook.

Launch into Word Analysis

Comparatives   Comparative words tell how two or more things compare to one another. There are three ways to compare. First, by adding an *er* ending to a word.

> **Examples:**   Jim is **taller** than Tim.
> Nan is **faster** than Jan.

The second way to compare is to use the words *more* or *less* before the word. You can also use the words *better* or *worse* to compare.

> **Examples:**   Jim is **more heroic** than Tim.
> Nan is **less shy** than Jan.
> Jim makes **better** pancakes.
> Nan had **worse** luck than Jan.

Work with a partner. On a separate sheet of paper, complete each sentence with the comparative form of a word.

1. It is _____ (hard) to be a hero than you think.

2. Emergencies are _____ (difficult) than normal situations.

3. Some people just respond _____ (good) to an emergency than others.

For more practice with comparatives, use page 52 of the Student Workbook.

Writing: Use a variety of organizational patterns, including comparison and contrast

Launch into Writing

Compare and contrast   Write a short essay using compare-and-contrast organization about two heroes whom you know about.

In your first paragraph, introduce the people you will compare and contrast. In your next paragraph, say how these people are similar and provide examples. In a third paragraph, point out a difference between the two people and provide examples for this also. Finish with a fourth paragraph that summarizes your comparison or draws a conclusion about the two people. Here's an example:

Study Tip

There are many reference books that list the different tenses and verb forms of regular and irregular verbs. If you are not sure what the past participle of a verb is, you can look in a reference book or ask your teacher.

Harriet Tubman and Calvin Fairbank were both heroes. Harriet made dangerous trips to rescue slaves. Calvin freed many slaves, even though he spent years in prison as punishment.

Harriet was born into slavery in the South. Calvin started preaching against slavery in New York.

Although Harriet and Calvin were different in some ways, they both worked to end slavery. They were both heroes.

For more practice comparing and contrasting, use pages 54–55 of the Student Workbook.

Writing: Use a variety of organizational patterns, including comparison and contrast

8

Before You Read

Background

In the last chapter you learned about different kinds of heroes. In this chapter, you will read an interview with a hero who works every day to make the world a better place. Do you know someone who is a hero like that?

LEARNING OBJECTIVES

- Evaluate evidence
- Use the past perfect tense
- Understand and use suffixes
- Write an article using supporting facts

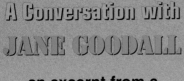

A Conversation with JANE GOODALL

an excerpt from a nonfiction book by Pat Cummings and Linda Cummings, Ph.D.

Building Your Vocabulary

1. Jane Goodall, the famous scientist you will read about, has always had a love of nature. Studying animals has involved difficulties for her. With a partner, decide if the phrases below reflect Jane's love of nature or the difficulties she faced. Write them in a chart like the one on page 89.

- fascinated with creepy, crawling things
- physically demanding
- a strong sense of self-discipline
- story of how a hen lays eggs
- go through thick, thorny places
- surrounded by lions and hyenas
- dreaming of going to Africa

Reading: Analyze text that is organized in chronological order

Love of Nature	Difficulties
fascinated with creepy, crawling things	*physically demanding*

2. Compare your charts with another pair's and discuss any differences.

Reading Strategy

Evaluate evidence   When you read nonfiction, you should evaluate information at all times. Writers often make claims. You need to judge whether or not these claims are valid. To make judgments, you need facts, data, reasons, and examples that support the claim. No author can provide *absolute* proof to back up claims. But authors *can* give enough evidence to allow you to decide whether the information they present is generally truthful or not.

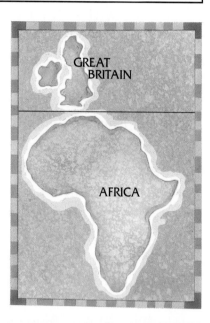

Applying the Reading Strategy

1. As you read, look for statements of opinion and other claims that the author makes. Write down each claim. Then look for evidence to support the claim.

2. Most evidence will come directly after the claim is made. The author may say, "Chimps need help," then give a list of reasons for *why* chimps need help. Your job is to evaluate those reasons. Do they make sense? Does the author support the reasons with facts, data, or other forms of evidence? Is the evidence *believable*?

3. To judge whether evidence is believable, think back to your own knowledge of the situation. Are the claims consistent with what you know? Can you think of any facts or reasons that disagree or disprove the claims?

4. At the end of the article, go over your list of claims and evidence. Did the author back up his or her claims? If so, then you can assume that the claims are probably true.

A Conversation with Jane Goodall 89

A Conversation with
JANE GOODALL

an excerpt from a nonfiction book by Pat Cummings and Linda Cummings, Ph.D.

I have been interested in animals since before I can remember. From the time I was very small, I was fascinated with creepy, crawling, furry, flying creatures. When I was quite young, my mother found me in my room with a handful of worms in my bed, watching as they went around and around. She didn't say, "Yuk!" and throw them out the window. She said, "Jane, if you leave them in here, they'll die. They need the air." And so I let them go free.

In fact, my mother is the most important reason for my doing what I've done and being who I've been. When I was four years old, I stayed on a farm, where I helped collect hens' eggs. I became puzzled and asked those around me, "Where is the hole big enough for the eggs to come out?" When no one answered to my satisfaction, I hid in a small, stuffy henhouse for four hours to find out. While I watched and waited, my mother looked frantically for me in the house and garden. She even called the police to help locate me. But when my mother saw me rushing toward the house in excitement, she didn't scold me for disappearing for so long. She sat down and listened to me tell the wonderful story of how a hen lays eggs.

Even my first books were about animals. I read *The Story of Dr.*

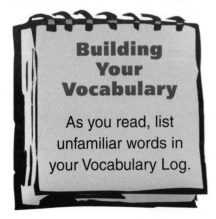

Building Your Vocabulary

As you read, list unfamiliar words in your Vocabulary Log.

Dr. Jane Goodall with a baby chimpanzee.

Reading: Determine the adequacy and appropriateness of the evidence for an author's conclusions

Louis Leakey.

Doolittle, The Jungle Book, and *Tarzan*. Looking back, I see that the original Tarzan was terribly hard on animals. But I didn't realize it then. Books are a great source of inspiration. They lure your mind to be imaginative. By the time I was eight or nine, I was dreaming of going to Africa. And my mother, a very special person, would say, "Jane, if you really want something and if you work hard, take advantage of opportunities, and never give up, you will somehow find a way."

In those days you had to learn a foreign language to get a scholarship to a university. But I couldn't do it—I couldn't speak French, couldn't speak German, couldn't speak Latin. So Mum said, "Why not take a secretarial course, then you can get a job anywhere in the world." So that's what I did.

But that didn't lead me directly to Africa. After I finished my secretarial class I began working for a documentary film company— a wonderful job, but with very low pay. When a school friend invited me to visit her family in Kenya, I readily accepted. I quit my job with the film company to begin work as a waitress in order to save the money. Finally, at age 23, with only enough money for boat fare to Africa (that was the cheapest way to travel in those days), I went off by myself to an unknown continent.

After two months in Africa I met the man who made all my dreams come true. Louis Leakey was an anthropologist and paleontologist who was interested in animals and early man. I made an appointment to meet him. Because I had studied animals throughout my childhood, I was able to answer many of his

As You Read

1. What role did Jane's mother play in helping Jane develop her interests?

anthropologist: a scientist who studies people, society, and culture

paleontologist: a scientist who studies fossils

lure: draw or attract

Reading: Determine the adequacy and appropriateness of the evidence for an author's conclusions

questions about the natural world, and he gave me a job as his assistant. I traveled with Louis and his wife, Mary, on one of their fossil-hunting expeditions to Olduvai Gorge. After some time, Louis decided I was the person he had been looking for to study the chimpanzees living near the shore of Lake Tanganyika, in what is now called Tanzania. And when the British authorities refused to let a young, untrained girl venture into the wilds of Africa on her own, who should volunteer to accompany me for the first three months but my own amazing mother.

And so my work began. After several years in Africa I returned to England to work for my Ph.D. in ethology from Cambridge University, and then I returned to the paradise of Gombe Stream, Tanzania, to continue my research.

How do you choose a project?

When I hear of chimps in need, in the wild or in captivity, I try to help. To raise money for my projects I sometimes give lectures and make appeals. Meanwhile, our research teams are in the field, monitoring

chimps we have identified and known for a while. In the wild chimps can live 40 to 50 years; in captivity they may live to be 60. We follow the different individuals. Every one has a unique life history.

What is a normal working day like for you?

In the field, every morning I would climb to my special peak with my binoculars, and a flashlight if needed, so I'd be ready when the chimps awoke. I recorded what I saw, sometimes even climbing into the treetops, whether I saw a chimp or not. It was marvelous. If it rained, I covered myself with a sheet of polyethylene. Sometimes it was very cold. I got extremely thin. When you follow the chimps, they

---

ethology: the study of animal behavior

polyethelene: a light plastic used in packaging

Reading: Determine the adequacy and appropriateness of the evidence for an author's conclusions

Dr. Jane Goodall with chimpanzees in Africa.

may go through thick, thorny, viney places. I often stopped to look at things because everything interests me, not just chimpanzees. You're in a magic world and if you rush through it, you lose it.

At times, a photographer or filmmaker joined me, but I usually went alone to observe the chimps quietly. Alone with the chimps, you can forget about humans. It's important not to disturb what the chimpanzees are doing because then you won't see them as they really are. I did try eating their food: fruit, leaves, and even insects. We do help if the chimps get sick. One chimpanzee, Gilka, allowed me to put antibiotics on her infected hand. If we seem non-threatening, then for the most part, the chimps will learn to trust us.

When I stay for three weeks at my home in England, I get up at 5:30 a.m. to get as much work done as I can. I eat breakfast, take the dog out, fix lunch, and have all afternoon for writing—books, letters, reports. I spend time with my family in the evening and then write late into the night.

Do you have any children? Is your family involved in your work?

When my son was born, I felt I'd learned a lot from the chimps about being a mother. I learned that it can be such fun. We had enormous fun. My son's name is Hugo, but his nickname is Grub. He was with me in Africa for his first nine years, then lived with my mother during his term time in England. Living in the Serengeti, surrounded by lions

As You Read

1. Does Dr. Goodall enjoy being a mother?

Reading: Determine the adequacy and appropriateness of the evidence for an author's conclusions

and hyenas, we kept an eye on Grub all the time. He grew up with my work but didn't get interested in it. He now lives in Tanzania, speaks Kiswahili, and is very African in his outlook.

When I first started my research, my mother joined me for the first three months in Tanzania because the British authorities wouldn't allow me to be on my own. She's still tremendously involved in my work. My sister came to help with photographs in the early days. And Grub's father, Hugo van Lawick, filmed hours of chimpanzee behavior in the early days as well.

What special preparations do you have to make for your work?

I used to go out into the field with a tape recorder and a pencil and paper. When I began my research, everything was new and I had to develop my own research methods. I had very little money in the early days. I took few clothes and ate very simply. I had curiosity, patience, and persistence. I was incredibly fit; not eating or drinking all day didn't bother me. And I always told someone roughly the direction I was going.

What is the hardest part of your work?

Getting funding is difficult. In the field, it's physically demanding to stay with the chimps and record information. You don't feel like getting up at 5 a.m. to go through a horrible thorny tangle, but you must follow the research plan you've set for yourself. Moreover, collecting data is fun, but you need it in a form you can analyze. You follow one individual all day and write

tangle: a mixed-up group of fibers

As You Read

1. What is the hardest part of Dr. Goodall's work?
2. How does Dr. Goodall feel about collecting data?
3. Why did the British authorities finally allow Dr. Goodall to go to Africa?

Reading: Determine the adequacy and appropriateness of the evidence for an author's conclusions

Dr. Jane Goodall at work.

details of his or her behavior, and then analyze the day later. It took a strong sense of self-discipline to go out, seven days a week, rain or shine or feeling ill. When I was in Kigoma, Tanzania, the British living there were shocked and said, "You must take Sunday off." I'd love to check my notes to see what I learned on Sundays!

Analyzing data is much harder than collecting it. But then even after seeing something a hundred times, you may suddenly realize: That's why they do it! It's a breakthrough. You light up inside. It's another kind of discovery.

What is left for you to explore?
The most exciting thing for future chimp studies is finding out how the different populations or communities across Africa vary. There are cultural variations. The sad thing is that, even as we speak, whole communities are being destroyed, so we will never learn how flexible their behavior is. We'll never learn about all of their different cultures, because many have already gone.

As You Read

1. How many days a week did Dr. Goodall work?
2. Which is harder, analyzing facts or collecting them?
3. What makes Dr. Goodall sad?

About the Authors
Pat Cummings and Linda Cummings, Ph.D.

Pat Cummings and Linda Cummings are sisters. Pat Cummings is the author of several books for young adults, including *Talking with Artists,* which is the winner of a *Boston Globe/Horn Book Award* and is an ALA Notable Book. Linda Cummings earned her Ph.D. in political science at the Massachusetts Institute of Technology.

A Conversation with Jane Goodall 95

Reading: Determine the adequacy and appropriateness of the evidence for an author's conclusions

After You Read

Retell It!

Work in groups. Because this is an interview, Dr. Goodall tells her story in first person, using words like "I" and "we." Retell the story using the third person, using words like "she" and "they." Write down your story and share it with the rest of the class.

Think, Discuss, Write

In pairs, discuss the answers to these questions. Then write them down.

1. **Recall details** How long can a chimp in the wild live? How long in captivity?

2. **Recall details** Who was Louis Leakey?

3. **Recall details** How does Jane Goodall label the chimps she works with? With names or numbers?

4. **Genre** Do you like having a question from the author and then having Dr. Goodall answer it? Why or why not?

5. **Genre** Do you think that having Dr. Goodall tell her story in her own words makes it more interesting or less interesting? Why?

6. **Connect main ideas** Do you think Dr. Goodall is a hero? Why or why not?

7. **Analyze cause and effect** Can you think of a question you would like to ask Dr. Goodall? What would it be?

Reading: Restate facts and details to clarify and organize ideas

What's Your Opinion?

Dr. Goodall tells a lot of stories in this reading. Which ones interested you the most? Which ones interested you the least? Work with a partner. For each numbered story from the reading below, place its number on a line like the one below. If it was very interesting, put its number on the right. If it was not very interesting, put its number on the left. If it was somewhat interesting, put its number in the middle.

Not very interesting ⟵———⟶ **Very interesting**

1. Dr. Goodall tells the story of having worms in her room as a little girl.

2. Dr. Goodall tells the story of hiding in the henhouse to watch a hen lay eggs.

3. Dr. Goodall tells the story of coming to Africa for the first time.

Launch into Grammar

The past perfect tense   The **past perfect** uses the verb *have* in the past tense with a second verb that has a past participle ending, often *ed*. The past perfect tense shows action that began and ended before some other past event occurred.

Written conventions: Identify and properly use past perfect verb tense

Example: Jane Goodall *had worked* for a film company before she met Dr. Leakey.

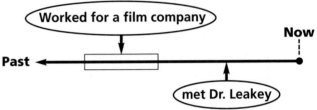

With a partner, write sentences using the past perfect tense of the verb in parentheses.

1. Before going to Africa, Dr. Goodall (study) at secretarial school.

2. Dr. Goodall's son Grub (live) in Africa for nine years before he went to England.

3. Before Dr. Goodall, no one (recognize) that chimps used tools.

 For more practice with the past perfect tense, use page 59 of the Student Workbook.

Launch into Word Analysis

Suffixes   Word endings that have special meanings are called **suffixes**. The suffix *ology* means "the study of." The suffix *ist* refers to a person. When you put these suffixes onto the end of root words, they take on a new meaning.

Example: *Bio* refers to life, so *biology* is the study of life.

A *biologist* is a scientist who studies life.

Reading: Know common roots and affixes derived from Greek and Latin and use this knowledge to analyze the meaning of complex words

Work with a partner to answer the questions on a separate sheet of paper.

1. *Geo* refers to the Earth, so what do we call the study of the Earth?

2. *Geo* refers to the Earth, so what do we call a scientist who studies the Earth?

3. *Archeo* refers to ancient things, so what do we call the study of ancient things?

4. *Archeo* refers to ancient things, so what do we call a scientist who studies ancient things?

Launch into Writing

Supporting facts   Whenever you state a conclusion or an opinion, it should be backed up with supporting facts. Your choice of facts is important. Make sure that each fact you include has a strong link to the conclusion or opinion that you stated.

Suppose Jane Goodall was coming to your school to speak. Write a newspaper article that explains who Goodall is and what she has to say about chimpanzees. Be sure that each statement is backed up with supporting facts.

For more practice with supporting facts, use pages 62–63 of the Student Workbook.

Reading: Distinguish between fact and opinion in expository writing

Persuade Your Classmates: Who Is the Greatest Hero?

In Unit 2, you read about different heroes:

- Chapter 5–The Big Friendly Giant and the boy's father who told the story
- Chapter 6–Two wonderful and loving mothers
- Chapter 7–Mother Teresa, Harriet Tubman, and many other courageous people
- Chapter 8–Jane Goodall

Work with a group of three classmates. Each member will choose a hero and give a speech to try to persuade the other members why that hero is the greatest of the three.

Step One: Plan Your Speech

A. Work in groups of three. Each person should choose a hero for their speech. Each member of the group needs to choose a different hero. You can choose a hero from the unit or another one you know about.

B. Write a short beginning for your speech. Include a brief description of the hero you chose and say that he or she is the greatest, for example:

I am going to talk to you about Harriet Tubman. She lived in the 1800s and worked saving people on the Underground Railway. I think you will agree that she is the greatest hero.

Hero: Harriet Tubman	
Actions and Accomplishments	**Qualities**
• escaped from slavery when she was 29 • rescued family and friends from slavery • served as a spy, scout, and nurse for the Union army • saved money for her trips to the South while working as a domestic	• *courageous* • *helpful* • *caring and hard-working* • *thrifty*

Writing: Write persuasive compositions: State a clear position on a proposal, support the position, anticipate and address concerns and counterarguments

C. Prepare a list of actions and accomplishments of your hero and what they show about the qualities of him or her. Make a chart like the one on page 100.

D. Practice presenting the information from your chart using sentences like this:

- She escaped from slavery when she was 29, which shows she was very courageous.

E. Prepare to finish your presentation by emphasizing that your hero is the greatest and that you hope your classmates will agree with you, for example:

- I know you will agree with me when I say that Harriet Tubman was the greatest hero.
- The facts clearly show that Harriet Tubman was the greatest hero.

Step Two: Practice Your Speech

Practice giving your presentation. Put all three parts together: your introduction, the points from the chart, and your finishing points. If possible, tape your presentation and listen to it. Did you speak clearly?

Step Three: Give Your Speech

Once you have practiced giving your presentation, get together with your group. Take turns presenting to each other. As you listen to other students' presentations, take notes about what you hear, to help you discuss or ask questions about it later.

Step Four: Evaluate Your Speech

After you have finished your presentation, invite your classmates to ask you questions or give you comments. Were they persuaded that your hero is the greatest? Use the Speaking Checklist on page 49 to comment on your classmates' presentations.

Record Your Speech

Record your presentation for a classroom listening lab. Listen to your own and others' tapes. Check out a tape to share at home or with another class.

Oral Conventions: Write and speak in complete, coherent sentences

Write an Expository Essay: What Makes a Person a Hero?

In Unit 2 you read about people who are heroes to many people. Not everyone agrees about who is a hero and who is not. Choose an individual from Unit 2 (or someone you know about) who you think is a hero. Then write a short expository essay that explains why that person is a hero. Follow the steps below to plan and write your essay.

1. Pre-write

Outline Your Essay Make a diagram like the one below. Start by writing the name of the hero in the largest circle. Next, think of the qualities that make the person a hero. Write these in circles below. Make sure you have included all qualities of your hero that you think are important. Your diagram may have more than two circles. Next, find supporting facts that strongly show how the hero has those qualities. Write these in boxes below each quality.

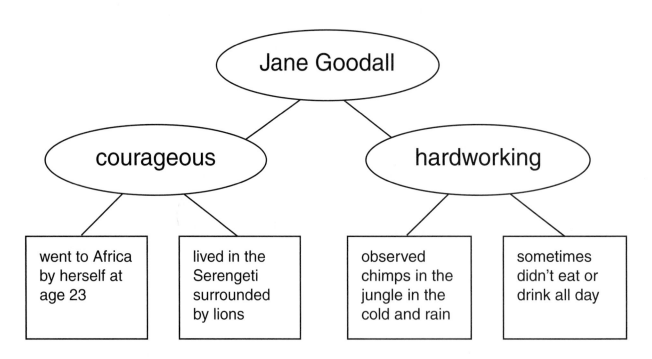

Writing: Write expository compositions: State the thesis, explain the situation, and offer evidence

2. Draft

A. Write your thesis statement and introductory paragraph

In the first paragraph you should put your thesis statement. It gives the main idea of your essay. Also in your first paragraph, refer to the main points you used to back up your thesis statement, but only in a brief way.

B. Write the topic sentences for each paragraph and then complete the paragraphs

The topic sentence of each paragraph gives a main point. It gives a quality of your hero. The rest of the sentences give facts to back up your topic sentence. These sentences tell why the person is a hero to you.

C. Write a concluding paragraph

Your last paragraph restates your thesis statement in a different way. It ties all of the important points you have made together. It emphasizes why the person is your hero.

3. Revise

Reread your draft and ask yourself these questions:

- Is my thesis statement clear?
- Have I used clear topic sentences for every paragraph?
- Have I backed up each topic sentence with supporting facts?

If you answer "No" to any of these questions, you will need to make changes to your essay to improve it. Work with a partner. Ask that person to answer the same questions about your essay. Make any additional changes based on your partner's feedback.

4. Edit and Proofread

Proofread your revised essay. Check punctuation, capitalization, and spelling. Look in the dictionary to verify spelling. Correct any errors you find.

5. Publish

Now you are ready to publish your expository essay. Create a final version on a computer or word processor. Double-space your essay so that it is easier to read. Use the spell-checking tool to look for any misspelled words. Finally, be sure to write your name, date, teacher's name, and the name of your class at the top of the page.

Writing: Revise manuscript to improve the focus by adding, deleting, clarifying, and rearranging words and sentences

A Hero's Welcome

Project Goal

Choose a hero you would like your town to celebrate. Create a poster for the celebration or festival. Include information about the events, food, and drink you will have.

1. Choose your hero. This person can be one of the heroes from the readings, a hero in your own life, or a hero you have made up! How can you reward this hero and celebrate the hero's accomplishments? Plan the celebration. Think about events, food, and drink that you will have.

2. Using the chart below as an example, create your own chart on a posterboard and list the name of the hero, the events, and the food and drink. Make sure to leave some space for pictures.

3. Provide some pictures for your poster. Get pictures from magazines or print ones out from the Internet that show events just like the ones you will have.

Words to Know

celebration	festival
award ceremony	event
parade	

Hero's name:	Rosa Parks
Events:	parade, speech, dinner
Food and Drinks:	roast chicken, mashed potatoes, green beans, lemonade

Writing: Write persuasive compositions: State a proposal, support the proposal with evidence, and anticipate concerns

Choose one or more of the following books to read. Write down in your Reading Log titles of the books you read and your opinion about each.

1. What facts are you learning as you read this book? How is the information organized?

2. Is this reading fiction or nonfiction? Do you like readings about true-life heroes or imaginary heroes better?

3. How did this book develop the theme of heroes?

4. Did you like this book? Why or why not? Give examples to support your opinions.

Nonfiction

So, You Want to Be President? by Judith St. George

This Caldecott Medal book's goal is to prove that all U.S. presidents were real people, not just "historical figures."

Only Passing Through: The Story of Sojourner Truth by Anne Rockwell

In 1843, a freed slave woman named Isabella decided to fight slavery. She renamed herself "Sojourner Truth," and dedicated herself to speaking out against slavery and oppression. This Coretta Scott King Illustrator Award book tells her story.

Fiction

The Folk Keeper by Franny Billingsley

In this Boston Globe-Horn Book Award winner, Corinna Stonewall is the Folk Keeper of the town of Rhysbridge, and her job is to keep the Folk, cave-dwelling gremlins, under control.

Miracle's Boys by Jacqueline Woodson

Ty'ree, Charlie, and Lafayette are three orphaned brothers raising themselves after their father drowns and their mother dies of diabetes in this Coretta Scott King Author Award winner.

Reading: Compare and contrast information on the same topic

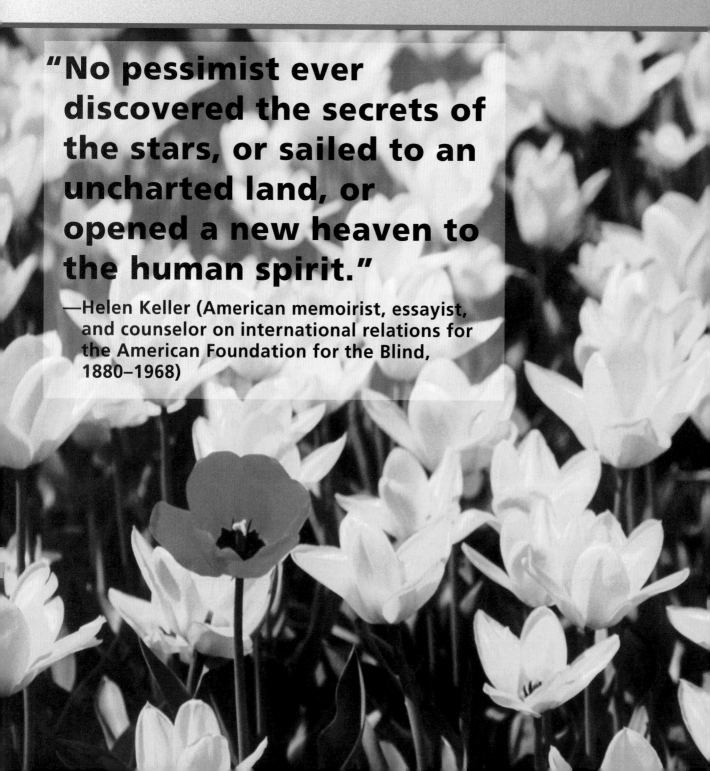

UNIT 3
Choices

"No pessimist ever discovered the secrets of the stars, or sailed to an uncharted land, or opened a new heaven to the human spirit."

—Helen Keller (American memoirist, essayist, and counselor on international relations for the American Foundation for the Blind, 1880–1968)

Discuss the Theme
Making Choices

In this unit, you will learn about different kinds of choices. In "Avalanche," you will learn about avalanches from experts. In "Seventh Grade" you will read about a boy who chooses to study French to impress a girl and ends up learning about human nature. In "Wringer," you will read about a boy named Palmer who does not believe in his town's tradition and how he must stand up for his beliefs. You will learn about an undersea explorer and the choices he had to make in "A Conversation with Robert Ballard." The choices we make every day can change us in many ways.

- What choices did you make today or yesterday?
- What difficult decisions have you made in the last year?
- Is it easy or difficult for you to make choices? Why?
- What are some good decisions you have made?

WRITING FOCUS:
Write a Research Report

9

Before You Read

Avalanche

an excerpt from a nonfiction book by Stephen Kramer

Background

Experts are people who have learned almost everything there is to know about a certain subject. The experts in "Avalanche" often have to make choices and decisions, and they help people to avoid places where avalanches might happen. In the nonfiction excerpt you are going to read, you will learn how experts decide if snow is safe or about to cause an avalanche.

LEARNING OBJECTIVES

- Identify and use features of media to find information
- Use commas and semicolons correctly
- Recognize words borrowed from other languages
- Research and take notes before writing

Building Your Vocabulary

How would you relate the phrases below to the time before or during an avalanche? Write the phrases in the correct place on a Cluster Map like the one on page 109.

sliding snow
unstable snow
break loose and slide
heavy snowfall

Reading: Use sentence and word context to find the meaning of unknown words

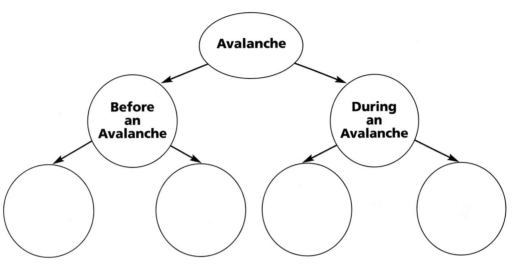

Reading Strategy

Identify media features and use them to find information Popular media include newspapers, magazines, and Internet sites. Each information medium has its own special features, but many features are common to some or all information sources.

Applying the Reading Strategy

1. As you begin to look over a source, first consider its title, subtitle, and author's name. Is this a source that you are likely to find useful?

2. Skim over the photos, maps, diagrams, graphs, and drawings to get an idea of the visual information that the source contains. Read some of the photo captions.

3. Look for headings, which are titles of particular sections within the source. What do these headings tell you?

4. As you read "Avalanche," pick out examples of various media features, such as title, subtitle, photos, and captions.

Reading: Identify the structural features of popular media and use the features to obtain information

AVALANCHE

an excerpt from a nonfiction book by Stephen Kramer

What Causes Avalanches?

People have not always understood why avalanches happen. Villagers living in the European Alps used to tell stories about evil spirits who lived high in the mountains. The spirits set off avalanches when they were angry. They rode the sliding snow down the mountain, dragging trees alongside to help them steer.

During the past fifty years, scientists have done many studies on avalanches. They have learned a great deal about how avalanches begin and why they happen more often in some areas than in others. This information is used to make decisions about safe places to put roads and buildings. Avalanche experts also use this information to help people avoid places where avalanche danger is high.

Unstable Snow

One of the best ways to learn more about avalanches is to study snow. Avalanche experts examine the different kinds of crystals in layers of snow. They pay close attention to how these crystals change over time. The experts use this knowledge to predict when and where avalanches are likely to begin.

Snow that is not sticking tightly to a hill, a mountainside, or other snow crystals is called

crystals: pieces of a substance that have become solid

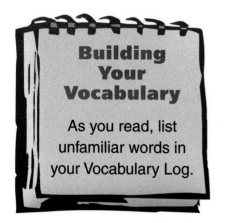

Building Your Vocabulary

As you read, list unfamiliar words in your Vocabulary Log.

As You Read

1. What does the title of this reading tell you? What is the topic of the reading?

2. What are the first two subtitles in the reading? What do they tell you about avalanches?

Reading: Identify the structural features of popular media and use the features to obtain information

unstable snow. The snow could begin sliding at any time.

Avalanche experts sometimes check for unstable snow by digging a snow pit. A snow pit is a hole dug down through layers of snow. The experts examine the pit's snowy sides. How hard is the snow in each layer? How well do the crystals in each layer stick together? Are there any layers that look as if they might break loose and slide? The answers to these questions help experts decide how stable the snow is and whether an avalanche is likely to happen.

After a heavy snowfall, the danger of an avalanche rises. The extra weight of the new

Villagers in the Alps, a European mountain range, used to think that evil spirits set off avalanches.

Reading: Identify the structural features of popular media and use the features to obtain information

As You Read

1. Read the captions and look at the photos. What do you find out about avalanches?
2. How can people cause an avalanche?

snow may trigger both slab and loose snow avalanches—especially in areas of unstable snow. A large snowstorm can set off dozens of avalanches within a few hours.

Although avalanches are more likely to happen after heavy snowfalls, waiting a day or two after a storm does not guarantee safety. People who travel in areas with unstable snow can cause avalanches any

Workers dig a snow pit and examine the sides of the pit to see if the snow is stable.

slab: something thick and flat

Reading: Identify the structural features of popular media and use the features to obtain information

An avalanche.

time—during, after, or between storms. The skiers, snowshoers, and snowmobilers who get caught in avalanches usually set off the snowslides that bury them. Most of these people could have stayed out of trouble by taking a safer route.

About the Author

Stephen Kramer

Stephen Kramer teaches elementary school in Vancouver, Washington. He did graduate work in biology and taught school on a Navajo reservation. He has also been a science researcher, a teacher, a writer, and a househusband. He has written several popular books for young readers about the world of science, such as *How to Think Like a Scientist*.

Reading: Identify the structural features of popular media and use the features to obtain information

After You Read

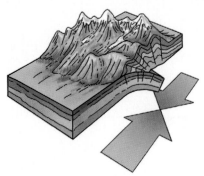

Shifting plates under the Earth's surface.

Retell It!

With a partner, retell the reading as a TV weather reporter would. Explain what causes an avalanche.

Think, Discuss, Write

In a small group, discuss your answers to these questions. Then write them down on a separate sheet of paper.

1. **Understanding words**   Define *unstable snow.*

2. **Cause and effect**   What is the best way to avoid getting caught in an avalanche?

3. **Analyze**   How did European villagers explain avalanches?

4. **Analyze**   What is the best way to learn more about avalanches?

5. **Cause and effect**   Why are features such as headings, photos, and captions helpful for understanding a nonfiction reading?

6. **Connecting main ideas**   What features of media would you include in a newspaper article about avalanches?

7. **Cause and effect**   Would you enjoy being an avalanche expert?

What's Your Opinion?

Write a paragraph with your reaction to "Avalanche." Include your opinions about the reading. Did you like it? Was it interesting? Would you recommend it to a friend? Post it along with your classmates' on a bulletin board.

Connecting to

Geography

Mountain ranges are formed when two of the Earth's plates push against each other, raising blocks of earth. The Alps in Europe, the Himalayas in Asia, the Rocky Mountains in the United States, and the Andes in South America are some of the highest and largest mountain ranges in the world.

Reading: Retell the central ideas of simple expository or narrative text

Launch into Grammar

Commas and semicolons Commas are used to make lists, to set off phrases, and to set off clauses. Take a look at how commas are used in these sentences.

1. Suddenly, the snow came down.
2. The snow was deep, heavy, and unstable.
3. Avalanches are dangerous, but they can usually be avoided.

In the first sentence, the comma sets off *Suddenly* from the rest of the sentence. In the second sentence, commas are used to separate items in a list. In the third sentence, a comma separates two independent clauses (clauses that can stand as complete sentences on their own) that are joined by a **conjunction** (such as *and, but, or*).

You can rewrite the third example above without a conjunction, replacing the comma with a **semicolon.**

4. Avalanches are dangerous; they can usually be avoided. (semicolon)

You can replace any conjunction that joins two independent clauses with a semicolon. Look at these examples, one with a conjunction and one with a semicolon.

5. Spring brings warm weather, and it also brings avalanches. (conjunction)
6. Spring brings warm weather; it also brings avalanches. (semicolon)

Written conventions: Use semicolons to connect independent clauses, and commas when linking two clauses with a conjunction

Study Tip

Often, reading a sentence aloud can help you decide where punctuation goes. Intonation often falls when you come to a comma, semicolon, or period. Try reading your sentences aloud with expression to help you recognize the pauses.

Write four sentences on a separate sheet of paper. In the first three sentences, use commas in the same way that they were used in examples 1–3 on the previous page. Follow example 6 for your fourth sentence—write a sentence that uses a semicolon.

For more practice with commas and semicolons, complete page 67 of the Student Workbook.

Launch into Word Analysis

Words from other languages English has borrowed a remarkable number of words from other languages. The word *avalanche* was borrowed from French. Other French words include *president, sentiment, establishment,* and *represent.* Spanish words that English has borrowed include *mosquito, pueblo,* and *rodeo.* The words *potato* and *tomato* were originally Native American, but they too came to English from Spanish.

What do all of the words borrowed from French have in common? The words borrowed from Spanish? With a partner, answer the following questions on a separate piece of paper. Explain each of your answers.

1. From what language would you guess that English borrowed the word *compliment*?
2. From what language would you guess that English borrowed the word *tornado*?

Reading: Recognize the origins and meanings of frequently used foreign words in English

Launch into Writing

Research information   To write his book, Stephen Kramer probably **researched** and took notes before he began to write.

Select a natural disaster or phenomenon that interests you, such as a tornado or an earthquake. Read two different sources about this phenomenon. Take notes about the causes and effects of the disaster on note cards.

Use the following example, which shows the start of some research, to help you create your own notecards.

Topic: *Forest Fires*
Source: *State of New Jersey, Forest Services Website*
Causes:
99% of all forest fires are set by people.
1. Arson - 52.9%
2. Child-related accidents - 14.6%
3. Smoking-related fires - 11.9%
4. Miscellaneous causes - 9.3%
5. Campfires (recreation) - 3.5%

For more practice researching for information, complete pages 70–71 of the Student Workbook.

Reading: Use various reference materials as an aid to writing.

10

Before You Read

Background

Sometimes we make choices without thinking about them. In this short story, a Mexican-American seventh-grader decides to study French because of a girl he likes. He impresses her, but his quick decision has unexpected results.

SEVENTH GRADE

**a story
by Gary Soto**

Building Your Vocabulary

This story includes some French words, and some made-up words. See if you can figure out which ones are French, and which ones are made up. Put words in the correct place on the chart on page 119.

Reading: Use context to resolve ambiguities about word meanings

bonjour   *may bien*   très bien   le bateau *el bat co*
Parlez-vous français? *ce j.* frenchie oh wewe gee
habbusted France
la me vava me con le grandma
ellame vaya up gillipolla el grandma

French	Made-up Language
le bateau	frenchie oh wewe gee

Compare your answers with a partner. Do you agree?

Reading Strategy

Support assertions with evidence from the text
When you read, you need to make assertions about what happens in the story. These assertions should not be made without evidence. Every conclusion you draw about why characters do something, think something, or say something should be supported with solid evidence from the text.

Applying the Reading Strategy

1. As you read, don't hesitate to make assertions about characters' thoughts, actions, or statements. You might even wish to jot down the important assertions you make.

2. Each assertion you make should be supported by evidence that you can point to in the text. For example, if you assert that one character likes another character, you should be able to point to specific evidence in the text.

3. Keep checking for additional evidence that supports your assertions as you read. Remember that events in the story could change the situation. If this occurs, you might need to change your assertions. If you *do* change your assertions, make sure that you have solid evidence to support them.

Reading: Make reasonable assertions about a text through accurate, supporting citations

stood = soportado
wobbly = tambaleante

a story by Gary Soto

On the first day of school, Victor stood in line half an hour before he came to a wobbly card table. He was handed a packet of papers and a computer card on which he listed his one elective, French. He already spoke Spanish and English, but he thought some day he might travel to France, where it was cool; not like Fresno, where summer days reached 110 degrees in the shade. There were rivers in France, and huge churches, and fair-skinned people everywhere, the way there were brown people all around Victor.

Besides, Teresa, a girl he had liked since they were in catechism classes at Saint Theresa's, was taking French, too. With any luck they would be in the same class. Teresa is going to be my girl this year, he promised himself as he left the gym full of students in their new fall clothes. She was cute. And good at math, too, Victor thought as he walked down the hall to his homeroom.

In homeroom, roll was taken, emergency cards were passed out, and they were given a bulletin to take home to their parents. The principal, Mr. Belton, spoke over the crackling loudspeaker, welcoming the students to a new year, new experiences, and new friendships. The students squirmed in their chairs and ignored him. They were anxious to go to first period. Victor sat calmly, thinking of Teresa,

bulletin: a brief news item

Reading: Make reasonable assertions about a text through accurate, supporting citations

who sat two rows away, reading a paperback novel. This would be his lucky year. She was in his homeroom, and would probably be in his English and math classes. And, of course, French.

The bell rang for first period, and the students herded noisily through the door. Only Teresa lingered, talking with the homeroom teacher.

"So you think I should talk to Mrs. Gaines?" she asked the teacher. "She would know about ballet?"

"She would be a good bet," the teacher said. Then added, "Or the gym teacher, Mrs. Garza."

Victor lingered, keeping his head down and staring at his desk. He wanted to leave when she did so he could bump into her and say something clever.

He watched her on the sly. As she turned to leave, he stood up and hurried to the door, where he managed to catch her eye. She smiled and said, "Hi, Victor."

He smiled back and said, "Yeah, that's me." His brown face blushed. Why hadn't he said, "Hi, Teresa," or "How was your summer?" or something nice?

As Teresa walked down the hall, Victor walked the other way, looking back, admiring how gracefully she walked, one foot in front of the other. So much for being in the same class, he thought.

herded: moved together as a group

As You Read

1. From what Teresa asks her homeroom teacher, what type of class do you think she is interested in?

2. Why does Victor blush when he speaks to Teresa?

Seventh Grade 121

The small, triangle-shaped campus bustled with students talking about their new classes. Everyone was in a sunny mood. Victor hurried to the bag lunch area, where he sat down and opened his math book. He raised his eyes slowly and looked around. No Teresa.

He lowered his eyes, pretending to study, then looked slowly to the left. No Teresa. He turned a page in the book and stared at some math problems that scared him because he knew he would have to do them eventually. He looked to the right. Still no sign of her.

Then he saw her. She was sitting with a girlfriend under a plum tree. Victor moved to a table near her and daydreamed about taking her to a movie. When the bell sounded, Teresa looked up, and their eyes met. She smiled sweetly and gathered her books. Her next class was French, same as Victor's.

They were among the last students to arrive in class, so all the good desks in the back had already been taken. Victor was forced to sit near the front, a few desks away from Teresa, while Mr. Bueller wrote French words on the chalkboard. The bell rang, and Mr. Bueller wiped his hands, turned to the class, and said, *"Bonjour."*

"Bonjour," braved a few students.

"Bonjour," Victor whispered. He wondered if Teresa heard him.

Mr. Bueller said that if the students studied hard, at the end of the year they could go to France and be understood by the populace.

Reading: Make reasonable assertions about a text through accurate, supporting citations

One kid raised his hand and asked, "What's 'populace'?"

"The people, the people of France."

Mr. Bueller asked if anyone knew French. Victor raised his hand, wanting to impress Teresa. The teacher beamed and said, *"Très bien. Parlez-vous français?"*

Victor didn't know what to say. The teacher wet his lips and asked something else in French. The room grew silent. Victor felt all eyes staring at him. He tried to bluff his way out by making noises that sounded French.

"La me vava me con le grandma," he said uncertainly.

Mr. Bueller, wrinkling his face in curiosity, asked him to speak up.

Great rosebushes of red bloomed on Victor's cheeks. A river of nervous sweat ran down his palms. He felt awful. Teresa sat a few desks away, no doubt thinking he was a fool. Without looking at Mr. Bueller, Victor mumbled, "Frenchie oh wewe gee in September."

Mr. Bueller asked Victor to repeat what he had said.

"Frenchie oh wewe gee in September," Victor repeated.

Mr. Bueller understood that the boy didn't know French and turned away. He walked to the blackboard and pointed to the words on the board with his steel-edged ruler.

"Le bateau," he sang.

bluff: to pretend to know something you do not know

As You Read

1. From reading the story, what do you think *bonjour* means?

2. Do you think Victor's classmates know he does not know French?

3. Why do you think Mr. Bueller guesses Victor does not know French?

Reading: Make reasonable assertions about a text through accurate, supporting citations

"Le bateau," the students repeated.
"Le bateau est sur l'eau," he sang.
"Le bateau est sur l'eau."

Victor was too weak from failure to join the class. He stared at the board and wished he had taken Spanish, not French. Better yet, he wished he could start his life over. He had never been so embarrassed. He bit his thumb until he tore off a sliver of skin.

The bell sounded for fifth period, and Victor shot out of the room, avoiding the stares of the other kids, but had to return for his math book. He looked sheepishly at the teacher, who was erasing the board, then widened his eyes in terror at Teresa who stood in front of him. "I didn't know you knew French," she said. "That was good."

Mr. Bueller looked at Victor, and Victor looked back. Oh please, don't say anything, Victor pleaded with his eyes. I'll wash your car, mow your lawn, walk your dog—anything! I'll be your best student, and I'll clean your erasers after school.

Mr. Bueller shuffled through the papers on his desk. He smiled and hummed as he sat down to work. He remembered his college years when he dated a girlfriend in borrowed cars. She thought he was rich because each time he picked her up he had a different car. It was fun until he had spent all his money on her and had to write home to his parents because he was broke.

sheepishly: in a shy and embarrassed way

Reading: Make reasonable assertions about a text through accurate, supporting citations

Victor couldn't stand to look at Teresa. He was sweaty with shame. "Yeah, well, I picked up a few things from movies and books and stuff like that." They left the class together. Teresa asked him if he would help her with her French.

"Sure, anytime," Victor said.

"I won't be bothering you, will I?"

"Oh no, I like being bothered."

"Bonjour," Teresa said, leaving him outside her next class. She smiled and pushed wisps of hair from her face.

"Yeah, right, *bonjour,*" Victor said. He turned and headed to his class. The rosebushes of shame on his face became bouquets of love. Teresa is a great girl, he thought. And Mr. Bueller is a good guy.

He raced to metal shop. After metal shop there was biology, and after biology a long sprint to the public library, where he checked out three French textbooks.

He was going to like seventh grade.

As You Read

1. Why doesn't Mr. Bueller say anything about Teresa's compliment to Victor?

2. Can you conclude that Teresa likes Victor? Why or why not?

wisps: small amounts of something

sprint: a short, quick run

About the Author

Gary Soto

The story "Seventh Grade" comes from Gary Soto's book of short stories called *Baseball in April.* Soto comes from a Mexican-American family. He did not have books to read when he was growing up, but, as a college student, he discovered poetry and literature. His other books include a collection of autobiographical essays, and *A Fire in My Hands,* a book of poems.

Reading: Make reasonable assertions about a text through accurate, supporting citations

After You Read

Retell It!

With a partner, tell the story from Teresa's point of view. What did she think about Victor in class and his use of French?

Think, Discuss, Write

Work in your same small groups and discuss your answers to these questions. Then write them down on a separate sheet of paper.

1. **Setting**   Where does Victor live?

2. **Draw conclusions**   Why does Victor decide to take French?

3. **Cause and effect**   If you were Victor and did not know French, what would you have done when Mr. Bueller called on you?

4. **Analyze characters**   Do you think that Mr. Bueller ever felt like Victor did?

5. **Understand plot**   Do you think that Teresa likes Victor?

6. **Predict**   Do you think Victor will help Teresa out with French?

7. **Make inferences**   What does Victor check out of the library? Why?

What's Your Opinion?

Work with a partner. Have you ever felt like Victor did? Make a Venn diagram like the one shown. List all the feelings that Victor felt under "Victor's feelings." Under "my feelings," list any feelings you

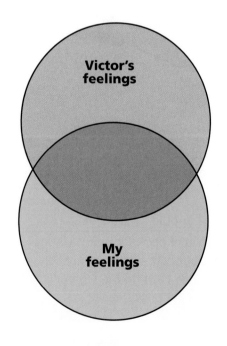

Reading: Recall major points in the text and make or modify predictions about forthcoming information

have felt but Victor did not. Put feelings where the circles overlap if you have both felt the same way.

Launch into Grammar

Spell *there, they're,* and *their* The words *there, they're,* and *their* are often confused. *There* is used to show the position of something. *They're* is a contraction of the words *they* and *are. Their* is a possessive adjective used to show that something belongs to two or more people.

You can tell which word to use from the context. Use *there* to point out the position of something. Use *they're* when where you would normally write *they are.* Finally, use *their* to show ownership of something by two or more people. Choose *there, they're,* or *their* to complete each sentence below. Write your answers on a separate sheet of paper.

1. The students in Victor's French class all brought _____ books to class.

2. "I saw Teresa over _____!" Michael said.

3. _____ going to have a party in French class at the end of the semester.

With a partner, reread the story, "Seventh Grade." Find as many examples of the words *there, they're,* and *their* as you can. Which word was used the most times in the story?

 For more practice with misspelled words, complete page 75 of the Student Workbook.

Study Tip

Sometimes, it helps to consider the part of speech. If two words sound the same, such as *it's* and *its,* it can be confusing to know which to use. To find out if you should use its or it's, try replacing the word with *it is.* If it does not fit, then you do not use an apostrophe.

Written conventions: Spell frequently misspelled words correctly

Launch into Word Analysis

Homophones and homographs Homophones are words that sound the same but differ in meaning. The words *there* and *their* are homophones. As you learned, *there* tells the position of something, while *their* shows ownership by more than one person. Words like *wear* and *where* are also homophones.

Homographs are words that are spelled the same, but have different meanings—like fall (the season) and fall (the verb).

With a partner, on a separate sheet of paper write down the meanings for each of the words below. Use the clues given.

1. duck (something you do)

2. duck (a bird)

3. stair (a thing)

4. stare (something you do)

After you finish the exercise above, look through "Seventh Grade" for other examples of homophones and homographs. How many can you find in the story?

 For more practice with homophones and homographs, complete page 76 of the Student Workbook.

Reading: Use knowledge of homophones and homographs to determine the meanings of words

Launch into Writing

Research questions   When you do research and take notes, it is helpful to write some **questions** that you have.

In "Seventh Grade," the main character, Victor, would like to travel to France. If you could travel, where would you like to go? What would you like to learn about this place? Write five research questions on note cards about the place. Then read about this place and take notes to answer your questions.

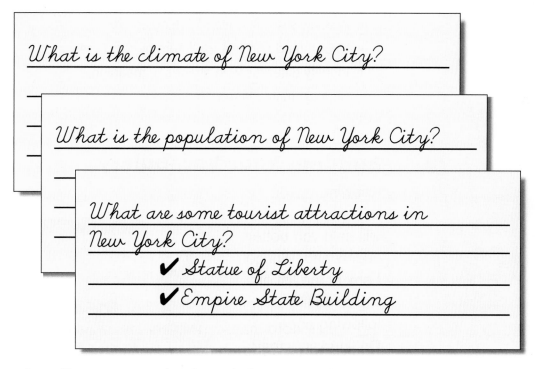

What is the climate of New York City?

What is the population of New York City?

What are some tourist attractions in New York City?
   ✔ Statue of Liberty
   ✔ Empire State Building

For more practice formulating research questions, complete pages 78–79 of the Student Workbook.

Writing: Write research reports by framing questions that direct the investigation

11

Before You Read

Wringer

**an excerpt from a novel
by Jerry Spinelli**

Background

Sometimes people have expectations of others. They think that other people should do certain things, just because they do them, or because other people their age do them. Part of growing up is learning to make choices on your own, no matter how hard they may be. In "Wringer," an excerpt from a novel, a young boy must make a difficult decision.

LEARNING OBJECTIVES

- Analyze the influence of setting on plot
- Understand and use the future perfect tense
- Identify differences in shades of meaning
- Support main ideas with details

Building Your Vocabulary

Knowing words that relate to pigeons will help you better understand "Wringer." Look at the list of words on the following page. Do you know their meanings? Look these words up in a dictionary and add them to your Vocabulary Log.

Reading: Use a dictionary to learn the meaning of unknown words

gobble
roosting
taste buds
passenger pigeon
gizzard
grind

Reading Strategy

Analyze the influence of setting on plot What happens in a story can sometimes depend on *where* it happens. A ghost story, for example, that takes place in a small, modern apartment would be very different from a ghost story set in a spooky old mansion. The story you are about to read takes place in a town that celebrates a Pigeon Festival every year, in which people practice their shooting skills on live pigeons. As you read "Wringer," keep in mind how much setting affects the outcome of the story's plot.

Applying the Reading Strategy

1. As you read, pay special attention to the setting of the story. What is special or unique about the place in which this story occurs?

2. Notice how events in the story are affected by where the characters live.

How would these characters act differently if they lived in a different town?

3. Keep the setting in mind as you get to the end of the story. How did the setting determine what happened to resolve the plot at the end of the story?

Reading: Analyze the influence of setting on the problem and its resolution

Wringer

an excerpt from a novel by Jerry Spinelli

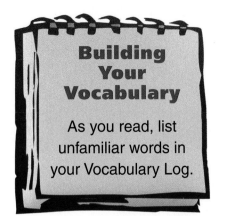

A pinch on his earlobe woke him. He opened one eye to find an orange button staring back. The pigeon was on his pillow, sounding like someone gargling water. Again it nipped his earlobe.

"Ow!"

Palmer swiped, and the bird flew to the foot of the bed. "I'm awake, okay?" Palmer wondered if his old pair of earmuffs was still around.

A knock at the door. His mother!

"Palmer."

"Yeah?" He threw his blanket over the pigeon.

"Time to get up."

True to her word, she did not come in.

"Okay. I'm up."

She went away.

The blanket moved like a ghost over his bed. He pulled it back. With a gobble, the pigeon flew off to the comic book stack. Like the day before, it skidded off the top comic and onto the floor. This bird, thought Palmer, is either dumb, clumsy, or a comedian. Palmer dressed and went down for breakfast. This time he returned not only with FrankenPuffs but Grape Nuts as well. He spread the cereal on the snow outside his window. The pigeon did not have to be coaxed. It flew out the window and attacked the food.

Over the next week Palmer got better acquainted with the pigeon and adjusted his own life to take his new friend into account. From the

coaxed: persuaded

Reading: Analyze the influence of setting on the problem and its resolution

library at school he borrowed a book about pigeons. Actually he sneaked it out. When it came to pigeons, he did not trust anyone in town. So he slipped the book into his bag and walked out as innocent-looking as possible. He had it back on the shelf in two days.

From the book he learned that pigeons go to sleep as soon as the sun goes down. This was called roosting. He learned that it was okay to feed his pigeon cereal, but that outside on its own it would probably eat some gravel. He learned that a pigeon isn't very fussy about what it eats, because its tongue has only thirty-seven taste buds.

He learned that a pigeon's heart is about the size of an acorn. And that a pigeon's heart, as measured against the size of its body, is one of the largest hearts in creation.

Palmer learned that in the wild pigeons used to live in the nooks and crannies of high rocky cliffs. When they came to this country, they headed for the things that looked like high rocky cliffs to them, which happened to be tall buildings and skyscrapers. And that's why pigeons live mostly in big cities.

He read about the passenger pigeon. Flocks of them numbered in the millions. So many were there that when they flew, they would block out the sun and people below would have to light torches. And then people began to shoot them. Even dynamite them. And by 1914 the last passenger pigeon was dead.

nooks and crannies: hidden corners and holes
flocks: groups of birds

As You Read

1. What is Palmer hiding in his room? Why is he hiding it?

2. What does Palmer take from the library? Why does he take it rather than check it out?

3. What are three things that Palmer learns about pigeons?

4. What happens to the passenger pigeons?

Wringer 133

There's something about pigeons, thought Palmer, that makes people want to shoot them. Whatever that thing was, he could not find it in the book.

He thought about a name. He thought about how the pigeon nipped his ear each morning. In fact, it was always nipping at something: the Nerf™ ball, the gray soldiers, book covers. So there it was: *Nipper*. And simply because Nipper sounded like a boy's name, "it" became "he."

Before long a routine had developed:

Wake up. (The "alarm clock" being nips on the earlobe.)

Pretend to be groggy when Mom knocks with official wake-up call.

Let Nipper out. Leave food on porch roof. (He had bought a box of Honey Crunchers, which he kept in his closet. He had studied cereal boxes and found out that Honey Crunchers contained a lot of fat; and fat helps keep a pigeon warm in winter, so said the book.)

Clean room. Leave no evidence of roommate.

Go to school (or, on weekends, out to play). Act normal. Return home. Let Nipper in.

Nipper walks up arm, stands on Palmer's head. Feels good. Nipper checks out room. Nipper skids off comic stack. Laugh. Play ball with Nipper. (Nipper would perch on the basket

groggy: tired

Reading: Analyze the influence of setting on the problem and its resolution

rim while Palmer tossed in Nerf™ ball shots. As the ball went by, Nipper nipped at it. Sometimes he caught it before it went through the net.)

Go to dinner. Return to find Nipper roosting.

Homework, read, TV. Go to closet, whisper "Good night, Nipper." Go to bed.

The hardest part of the routine came each day when he left the house: *Act normal.* How was he supposed to act normal in a town that murdered pigeons?

Boom

The first bird emerged from the freshly stocked white box, new shooter shooting.

The kid swung and pointed. "Pow! Pow!" And kept jabbering at Palmer. "And then I'll be—"

Boom

"Pow!—a wringer. I'm gonna wring their—" He tried to show what he would do but spilled purple slush over his own wrist.

Boom

"Pow! Pow! I'm gonna wring more than anybody. I'm gonna—"

Boom

"Pow! I'm gonna—"

Palmer was no longer hearing the yammering kid. He was looking up. The second

jabbering: talking very fast
yammering: babbling

As You Read

1. Who is Nipper?
2. What does Palmer do to keep Nipper a secret?
3. What is the hardest part of Palmer's routine? Why?

Reading: Analyze the influence of setting on the problem and its resolution

pigeon out of the box had been another Nipper look-alike. It took a few casual steps and stopped to peck at the ground, a perfect target. Incredibly, the shooter had missed. The pigeon had taken off and was now higher than the afternoon sun. Another rare one, a miracle bird.

Blocking the sun with his fist, Palmer watched the bird circle the field, as the others had done. Palmer's shoulder muscles flexed to the rhythm of its wings, urging it on. It circled a fourth time. And again. It was not leaving. It was simply circling, circling. In fact, impossibly, *it seemed to be getting closer.*

It was Nipper.

Palmer simply and suddenly knew it.

And just as suddenly the horror of what he was doing struck him. For if Nipper truly was searching for him—and found him—

Palmer's own stupid, unthinking, upturned face was nothing more than bait luring his pigeon back to a second chance at death. This time the shooter would not miss.

Palmer covered his face with his hands. *No,* he prayed, *No No No. . . .*

Too late.

As the bird broke from its circle and began its long downward swing, the little kid beside Palmer pointed and screamed, "Look! It's coming back! It's coming back!" Palmer knocked the water ice from the kid's hand as the people

bait: something used to lure an animal
water ice: cold, icy drink

Reading: Analyze the influence of setting on the problem and its resolution

began to look up. Fingers pointed, more faces turned. The shooter, who had been walking away, stopped and turned. His hand dipped into the pocket of his vest. The only sound was the outraged howl of the purple-plastered kid.

Palmer stepped away from the people then, into the clear, onto the shooting field, the better to be seen, for he knew now that there was no stopping it. Downward came the bird, lazily looping through the haze, gray in gray descending, gliding, a summer sledder down a slope of sunsmoke.

And landed on Palmer's head.

At that point even the howling kid shut up. His boggling eyes joined a townful of others aimed at a spot just above Palmer's forehead. Nipper's toes clutched and moved on his scalp, and for a strangely wonderful moment he felt himself crowned.

in the clear: free from obstructions
crowned: with something placed on the head as a mark of victory

As You Read

1. In this part of the story, it is Pigeon Day. What happens to the second bird that comes out of the box? Which bird is it?
2. Why does Nipper come back? How does this make Palmer feel?
3. Where does Nipper land?

About the Author
Jerry Spinelli (b. 1941)

Jerry Spinelli was born in Norristown, Pennsylvania. He wrote *Who Put That Hair in My Toothbrush?* and *Maniac Magee*, which won the 1991 Newbery Award. In 1998, *Wringer* was named a Newbery Honor book.

Reading: Analyze the influence of setting on the problem and its resolution

Retell It!

Work in pairs. Summarize the story using five or more sentences.

Think, Discuss, Write

Work in the same small groups and discuss your answers to these questions. Then write them down.

1. **Recall details** What things does Palmer do to keep Nipper a secret?

2. **Make inferences** What is the hardest part of Palmer's daily routine?

3. **Analyze** How do you think the people of the town felt when Palmer rescued Nipper?

4. **Make inferences** Where is Nipper at the end of the story? How does this make Palmer feel?

5. **Setting** How important is the setting in this story? Why?

6. **Discuss** Do you think Palmer was wrong to make Nipper a pet? Why?

7. **Predict** How do you think the book ends?

Reading: Retell the central ideas of simple expository or narrative text

What's Your Opinion?

Work with a partner. Which of these would be hard for you to do? Why?

- hide a pigeon in your room
- sneak a book out of the library
- learn about pigeons
- take care of a pigeon
- keep your interest in pigeons a secret

Launch into Grammar

Future perfect tense   Like the present perfect and past perfect, the **future perfect** tense uses a form of the verb *have* with a second verb that has a past participle ending, usually *ed.* The **future perfect** uses **will have** to describe the length of a future action or state by a future date or time.

By June, Nipper *will have lived* with Palmer for three months.

On Tuesday, Palmer's library books *will have been* two days overdue.

Both sentences show how long a future action or state continued by a future date. In the first sentence, for example, one future action, Nipper living with Palmer for three months, will have continued for three months by June.

Writing Tip

Remember that the future perfect tense has a very specific use. It tells what will happen by when—a certain time in the future. Clues that future perfect tense is needed are phrases like **By this date, By this time tomorrow, By next year.**

Reading: Identify and properly use the future perfect tense

With a partner, complete each sentence using the future perfect tense of the verb in parentheses. Write your answers on a separate sheet of paper.

1. By the end of high school, Nipper _____ (stay) with Palmer for years.

2. By the day of the Pigeon Festival, many visitors _____ (arrived) in town.

 For more practice with the future perfect tense, complete page 83 of the Student Workbook.

Launch into Word Analysis

Shades of meaning   The words *softly* and *quietly* can sometimes have similar meanings:

   It rained *softly*.

   It rained *quietly*.

   However, if you change the situation, the same two words cannot be used.

   She kicked the ball *softly*. (makes sense)

   She kicked the ball *quietly* at the goal. (doesn't make sense)

   With a partner, decide whether one or both of the words in parentheses can be used in the sentences below. Write your answers on a separate sheet of paper.

1. He _____ the ball. (tossed, threw)

2. She _____ and turned all night. (tossed, threw)

Reading: Understand and explain "shades of meaning" in related words

Launch into Writing

Write an outline   An outline summarizes the major topics you will address in your writing. Outlines use a system of letters and numbers to organize the information they contain. Use Roman numerals (I, II, III, IV, etc.) to identify major topics. Under each major topic, indent and use capital letters (A, B, C, D, etc.) to identify subtopics. Under each subtopic, indent and use Arabic numerals (1, 2, 3, 4, etc.) to identify particular pieces of information.

I. Physical characteristics of pigeons
  A. Roosting
  B. What pigeons eat
    1. Feeding a pigeon cereal
    2. What pigeons eat on their own
  C. Size of a pigeon's heart
    1. Actual size
    2. Heart size in relation to body size

II. Types of pigeons
  A. Wild pigeons
    1. Where they live in the wild
    2. Why they are attracted to cities
  B. Passenger pigeons
    1. Number of passenger pigeons
    2. Reason people killed them off

With a partner, choose a common animal and find a book or an article about that animal. Write an outline of what you learn from that book or article.

 For more practice writing outlines, complete pages 86–87 of the Student Workbook.

Reading: Clarify an understanding of texts by creating outlines, logical notes, summaries, or reports

12

A Conversation with

ROBERT BALLARD

an excerpt from a nonfiction book by Pat Cummings and Linda Cummings, Ph.D.

Before You Read

Background

In school, people begin to make choices about the kinds of careers that interest them. These choices help prepare them for the future. In "A Conversation with Robert Ballard," a nonfiction text, you will learn what choices Robert Ballard made along the way to becoming a deep-sea explorer.

LEARNING OBJECTIVES

- Find supported assumptions and arguments
- Use colons
- Use prefixes to guess word meanings
- Write a bibliography

Building Your Vocabulary

1. There are many scientific words in this reading. They relate to life under the sea and to science in general. In a small group choose one of the following prefixes or suffixes. Then

Eel

Reading: Use knowledge of prefixes to determine the meaning of words skim the reading. How many words beginning with that prefix or suffix can you find? Copy the chart below on a separate sheet of paper. Make a complete list for your group by filling out the chart. Try to find other words with prefixes like *hydro-* and *sub-*.

Prefix or Suffix	Words from story with that prefix or suffix
ex-	expedition
-ogy	biology

2. Now compare your list with the list from another group. Did you miss any words? What do you think each prefix or suffix means?

Reading Strategy

Find supported assumptions and arguments
When an author tries to persuade you to believe something, his or her opinions should be supported with facts.

Applying the Reading Strategy

1. As you read, write down specific opinions that Robert Ballard has.

2. Write down what he says about these beliefs and how he supports them.

3. With a partner, compare the opinions you have found and how Robert Ballard supports them.

Reading: Identify text that uses sequence or other logical order

A Conversation with
ROBERT BALLARD

an excerpt from a nonfiction book by Pat Cummings and Linda Cummings, Ph.D.

Building Your Vocabulary

As you read, list unfamiliar words in your Vocabulary Log.

My love affair with the sea began when I was no more than six years old, walking along the sandy beaches of Southern California. I always wanted to make the first set of footprints in the wet sand. My adventures began in small tidal pools carved in the rocks where creatures of all colors and shapes hid from view or darted back and forth, eager for the rising tide to set them free. Later my adventures took me out on a long pier near my home, where I spent countless hours dangling a baited hook beneath the sea, wondering what monster I might catch.

Unlike many surfers who sought the perfect wave, my interests always lay beneath the sea's surface in a world I could only imagine and dream of. Soon, wearing a snorkel and a mask, I made my first solo adventures in the deep. Later I would learn how to scuba dive, expanding my world of exploration many times over. All along the way, my parents and teachers encouraged my interest in the sea, providing me with books to read or taking me to the ocean once we moved inland and I couldn't reach it by myself.

Perhaps the greatest turning point in my life came when I was in high school and I wrote a letter to the famous Scripps Institution of Oceanography, in San Diego, asking how I might learn more about the sea.

A kind scientist answered my letter and told me how to apply to Scripps for a summer scholarship,

tidal pool: a small body of water beside an ocean
baited: hung with food to catch fish
snorkel: a tube used to breathe underwater
inland: toward the interior of a country

Robert Ballard.

Reading: Identify text that uses sequence or other logical order

which I received. During one of their cruises that summer, I met Dr. Robert Norris, a marine geologist. He loved the sea almost as much as I did. His passion was infectious. Soon he was asking me what my plans were and where I expected to attend college. I told him I didn't know, so he suggested I consider his school, the University of California in Santa Barbara.

My parents drove me to Santa Barbara for an interview, and one year later I drove there myself, this time as a member of the freshman class.

Now my love affair with the sea became a serious endeavor. If I wanted to be an undersea explorer, I needed to learn as much as I could about the laws of the physical world that controlled the environment I wanted to enter. The undersea world is not our natural world. It is unforgiving to those who make mistakes. At its greatest depths the water temperature is near freezing, the pressure is eight tons per square inch, and it is totally dark. It is easy to get lost in such a world. I needed to learn a lot about geography, navigation, meteorology, geology, biology, and many other things. While I was in school, I took a little of everything.

I decided another important thing for me to do was to join the U.S. Navy. If I was going to be an undersea explorer, I would have to

marine geologist: a scientist who studies underwater rocks

physical: having substance or material

As You Read

1. When does Robert Ballard's love affair with the sea begin?

2. What is the greatest turning point in his life? How does this change his life?

3. How can the deep sea be dangerous to people who make mistakes?

4. What subjects does he need to study?

5. Why does he decide to join the Navy?

Ocean explorers placing exploration gear in the water.

A Conversation with Robert Ballard 145

A submersible.

lead men and women on dangerous adventures where they might get hurt, and I didn't want that to happen. In the Navy I learned discipline, organization, and how to motivate and lead people on expeditions so that we could explore the wonders of the deep.

Finally, the time came to put all that I had learned to use, to go forth with a team of men and women and explore—an adventure I am still on and hope to be on for many years to come.

What was the scariest thing that ever happened in your work?

I have had many scary moments—a fire in my submersible at 9,000 feet, or crashing into the side of a volcano at 20,000 feet. But perhaps the scariest experiences are when someone on my team is in danger: trapped in an undersea fissure or entangled in cables on a wreck. My profession can be dangerous. One must never take needless risks. Never tempt Neptune, the god of the sea, too far.

How do you choose a project?

I ask myself, is the project challenging? Has it ever been done before? Is it truly worth doing? Does it have importance to the world? I follow my own ideas and work on projects that I'm passionately interested in. Reading and research generate ideas for me.

Where do you work?

When I'm not at sea, I work at the Institute for Exploration in Mystic, Connecticut, where we are building a research center and public exhibition

submersible: a small underwater craft used for research

fissure: a crack in the earth's surface

Reading: Identify text that uses sequence or other logical order

A submersible aboard the research vessel Discovery.

center, including a deepwater aquarium, which will open in March 1999. I also have an extensive library at home, where I research topics in maritime history, archaeology, and oceanography that interest me and that relate to my work.

What is a normal working day like for you?

When you are working at sea, it is on a 24-hour basis. Your crew is standing three shifts of four hours on and eight hours off duty. As expedition leader, your job is to be awake, alert, and ready to make important decisions anytime, day or night. When it gets hot and heavy, you learn to survive on little sleep. You learn to catnap under all kinds of conditions.

What special preparations do you have to make for your work?

I need to assemble a dedicated team who shares my passion and has the knowledge and motivation to operate extremely complex technologies under the worst of conditions.

What is the hardest part of your work?

The hardest thing about my work is to convince people to sponsor an expedition—finding a Queen Isabella who'll hock her jewels and trust in my dream.

As You Read

1. What is the scariest experience Ballard has had?

2. Where does he work when he is not at sea?

3. Why does he have to be able to survive on little sleep?

4. What is the hardest thing about Robert Ballard's work? Why?

aquarium: a container where aquatic animals are kept

maritime: having to do with the sea

archaeology: the study of human life in the past

catnap: very short period of sleep

hock: to sell

Reading: Identify text that uses sequence or other logical order

What was your biggest discovery?

My biggest discovery was the luxury liner Titanic, in the North Atlantic, but I am most proud of discovering hydrothermal vents and ancient Roman trading ships.

The hydrothermal vents, deep-sea hot springs that are formed when plates of earth move apart on the ocean floor and crack open in the crust, support truly amazing communities of undersea animals. Most of the creatures my colleagues and I found were completely new to science. We stored specimens in everything from Tupperware to plastic bags to take back for study.

What is left for you to explore?

My next project is one that National Geographic is sponsoring on the Battle of Midway. Right now I'm heavily involved with the research for this project and with assembling my team. Then, using a nuclear submarine that can go 3,000 feet below the surface—and hover or move along the ocean floor on special tires for more than a month—I plan to search for ancient shipwrecks in the eastern Mediterranean.

Finding at least one shipwreck from each century would provide such a fascinating, complete historical panorama . I plan to

plates: theoretical sections of the earth which float on and travel over earth's core

specimens: animals collected as typical examples of their kind

panorama: a wide view or perspective

History

This reading mentions two historic events. One is the sinking of the *Titanic*. It was a luxury passenger ship that hit an iceberg on its first voyage in 1912. It had been advertised by its owners as "unsinkable." More than 1500 people of the 2200 who were on board died in the accident.

The other historical event Robert Ballard refers to is Queen Isabella of Spain financing Columbus's trip to the New World. He went to the court of Queen Isabella and King Ferdinand to ask for money to pay for his exploration. The queen raised funds for him by borrowing money against the value of her jewels. The rest is history!

Reading: Identify text that uses sequence or other logical order

spend the next several years searching the deep sea for lost pages in our ancient history, stories locked in the cold, dark depths of Davy Jones's locker. All told, I've completed over 110 expeditions.

As You Read

1. What is Robert Ballard's biggest discovery?

2. How would finding a shipwreck from each century provide important historical information?

3. How many expeditions had he completed at the time of the interview?

A sunken ship.

Davy Jones's locker: a sailor's phrase for the bottom of the ocean

About the Authors

Pat Cummings

Pat Cummings and Linda Cummings are sisters. Pat Cummings is the author of several books for young adults, including *Talking with Artists*, which is the winner of a *Boston Globe*/Horn Book Award and is an ALA Notable Book.

Linda Cummings, Ph.D.

Linda Cummings earned her Ph.D. in political science at the Massachusetts Institute of Technology. She has worked extensively as an editor and researcher.

After You Read

Retell It!

With a partner, take the roles of the interviewer and Robert Ballard. Retell the reading by conducting the interview.

Think, Discuss, Write

Work in pairs and discuss your answers to these questions. Then write them down.

1. **Retell**   Where is Scripps Institution of Oceanography located?

2. **Retell**   Describe the cycle of Ballard's projects.

3. **Analyze**   Does Robert Ballard support most of his arguments and assumptions with facts?

4. **Connect main ideas**   Why is Robert Ballard's work important?

5. **Cause and effect**   Is it important in nonfiction writing to support assumptions with facts?

6. **Interpret** How would you prepare for a career like Robert Ballard's?

7. **Connect**   Would you be interested in a career like Robert Ballard's? Why?

What's Your Opinion?

With a partner, give your reactions to this reading. Use a separate sheet of paper to write down the things about Robert Ballard's job that you think would be exciting or fun. Write down the things that you think would be scary or not much fun.

Reading: Determine the adequacy and appropriateness of the evidence for an author's conclusions

☺ (fun, exciting)	☹ (not fun, scary)
riding in a submersible	*being in danger*

Launch into Grammar

Colons   A colon is used to introduce a list of items. Colons are also used to introduce an example, explanation, or a restating of a sentence. Here are some examples:

> In school, Ballard had to learn about: geography, navigation, meteorology, geology, biology, and many other things.

> Ballard's love of the ocean started early: as a boy he spent countless hours on a pier near his home.

Rewrite each of these short paragraphs as a single sentence with a colon.

1. In the Navy, Ballard learned many things. He learned discipline. He learned organization. He learned how to be a leader.

2. As an expedition leader, Ballard needs to do many things. He needs to be alert. He needs to be awake. He needs to be ready to make important decisions at any time.

   With a partner, write four sentences that include a colon.

Written conventions: Use a colon to introduce a list

Launch into Word Analysis

Prefixes   A prefix is a part of a word that can be put together with a word root to form a new word. Prefixes always come *before* the word root. The prefix *un-* means "not." When added to the beginning of a word root, the new word created with *un-* generally has the opposite meaning of the word root itself.

With a partner, find meanings for the following words.

Reading: Use knowledge of prefixes to determine the meaning of words

Word root	Word
cover	uncover
comfortable	uncomfortable
afraid	unafraid
beaten	unbeaten
fair	unfair

Launch into Writing

Write a bibliography   A **bibliography** lists the source materials you use in a report in alphabetical order. Do a research report on the Titanic. Write a bibliography that contains five sources. Follow these guidelines to prepare a bibliography:

A typical listing for a book is written like this:

Author's last name, first name, middle initial. *Title.* City where book is published: Publisher, Copyright date.

Example: Wade, Wyn Craig. *The Titanic: End of a Dream.* New York: Rawson Wade, 1979.

A listing for a magazine is written like this:

Author's last name, first name, middle initial. "Title of the article." *Title of the magazine.* (Month Year): page numbers of the article.

Example: Garzke, W. H. and Brown, D. K. "How did the Titanic really sink?" *Naval History Magazine* (September 1996): pp. 15–19.

 For more practice writing a bibliography, use pages 94–95 of the Student Workbook.

Writing: Quote or paraphrase information sources, citing them appropriately

Give an Interview About Choices

In Unit 3, you read selections about choices:

- Chapter 9–an article about difficult choices experts have to make in the event of an avalanche

- Chapter 10–a short story about choices a seventh grader makes in order to get a girl's attention

- Chapter 11–an excerpt about a boy who makes a choice about standing up for his pet pigeon in a town dangerous to pigeons

- Chapter 12–an interview about choices that a famous deep-sea explorer has to make about his career

Form four small groups, each focusing on the choices made by one of the following:

- Avalanche experts from "Avalanche"
- Victor from "Seventh Grade"
- Palmer from "Wringer"
- Robert Ballard from "A Conversation with Robert Ballad"

Each group will conduct an interview with their group's character or individual. One group member will take the role of the character or individual

and another will be the interviewer. All group members will help draft questions for the interviewer to ask, as well as answers the interviewee (person being interviewed) will give. The questions should be about choices each had to make.

Step One: Plan Your Interview

List choices the person or character had to make. Make up questions that the interviewer can ask about these choices. Write down answers the person or character can give. Discuss these. Write down notes on note cards that the interviewer and interviewee can use for the interview. Decide where you'll give your interview—at a local library, on TV, on a radio talk show, etc.

Step Two: Practice Your Interview

All group members should read the checkpoints in the Speaking Checklist first. The interviewer and interviewee should use the note cards to practice delivery, keeping the checkpoints in mind. Other group members—the audience—should provide feedback based on the checkpoints. Keep in mind who your audience will be—radio listeners, TV watchers, etc.

Step Three: Present Your Interview

Now you are ready to present your interview to the rest of the class who will act as your audience.

Step Four: Evaluate Your Interview

Each group member should evaluate the interview by commenting on the checkpoints in the Speaking Checklist. How can you improve your interview?

Record Your Interview

Record your interview for a classroom listening lab. Listen to your group's and other groups' recording. Check out an interview to share at home or with another class.

Speaking Checklist

✔ Use appropriate tone of voice. Interviewers who ask the questions should use a rising tone of voice at the end of questions. Interviewees should answer with a confident voice about choices they had to make.

✔ Try to make eye contact with members of your audience. Don't get distracted by your notes. Just use them for reference.

✔ Listen carefully so that you don't interrupt each other. Pause before asking and answering each question. This lets your audience focus on the question and the answer.

✔ Ask for clarification if you don't understand the interviewer's questions or the interviewee's answers.

✔ Try to make eye contact with people in your audience.

✔ Pronounce your words clearly and correctly.

Write a Research Report: Making Choices

Think about which reading interests you most. Would you like to learn more about avalanches, pigeons, the culture and language of the French people, or undersea exploring? You will write a research report on one of these topics. Decide what interests you most about the topic. Would you like to be an avalanche expert or undersea explorer? You could research what it would take to be one. Would you like to raise pigeons? Would you like to visit France? What would it take? Here's an example of the beginning of a report:

Undersea Exploring

Exploring the sea and all the plant and animal life that lives in the ocean would be a fascinating job.

To have a career working as a marine biologist or geologist a person must learn a lot about geography, navigation, meteorology, geology, biology, and many other things.

If you choose to devote your life to the sea, you must study very hard. You would spend much of your life away from your family and friends, traveling and studying.

To write your research report, follow these steps:

1. Pre-write

Before you begin researching your topic, think about the structure of your report. How many paragraphs will you have? How many main ideas do you want to include? Organize the facts and details by taking notes on note cards and writing an outline.

2. Draft

Follow these steps to organize your research report.

A. Introduce your topic in the first paragraph.

B. Organize your main ideas. Write one paragraph about each.

C. Supply supporting details. Add details to support each main idea.

D. End with a summary.

Refer to your outline as you draft your research report.

3. Revise

Reread your draft and ask yourself these questions:

A. Have I introduced my topic effectively?

B. Does the order of my main ideas make sense?

C. Do I need to add more facts or details?

D. Have I summarized my main ideas?

Consider your answers to these questions as you revise your research report. Ask a classmate to read your report and answer these same questions.

4. Edit and Proofread

Proofread your revised report. Check punctuation, capitalization, and spelling. Look in a dictionary to verify spelling.

5. Publish

Create a multimedia presentation, using drawings, diagrams, video, slides, or music to support your report. Present your report to the class.

Talk Show with a Panel of Experts

Project Goal

You are appearing on a television show that has a panel of experts. These experts discuss specific current events. They discuss the different problems we are facing today and what choices we must make to solve them. During the discussions, the panelists often disagree with each other!

1. Work in groups of five. One person will be the moderator. The moderator keeps the discussion going and calls on the experts to speak. The other people will be the experts.

2. Choose a topic for your experts to discuss. Here are two ideas: year-round school, and why children need to exercise more.

3. Divide the experts into pairs. Decide on two different ways, or choices, you can use to deal with your topic. One pair will present one choice, and the other pair will present the other choice.

4. The expert panelists research the topic. They go to the library, or look up information on the Internet. They write down reasons that support their choice of how to solve the problem. The moderator writes down questions to ask both groups. The moderator will ask these questions throughout the discussion.

5. Tape record or videotape your television show. The moderator should start the program with a brief summary of the issue and who the guests are. He or she will then call upon panelists to present their point of view. Panelists present facts to support their reasons. Panelists may comment on each others' opinions and supporting facts until the moderator tells them it is time to move on.

6. Watch your video or listen to the tape of your television show. See how you can improve your role.

7. Perform your television show for the rest of the class.

Words to Know

panel	current events
panelist	moderator
experts	choices

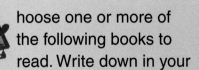

hoose one or more of the following books to read. Write down in your Reading Log titles of the books you read and your opinion of each. Ask yourself these questions:

1. Is this book fiction or nonfiction? Do you prefer to read fiction or nonfiction? Why?

2. How does this book develop the theme of choices?

3. Did you like this book? Why or why not? Give examples to support your opinion.

Nonfiction

The Circuit, Stories from the Life of a Migrant Child by Francisco Jiménez

These stories, which received the Boston Globe-Horn Book Award, are based on the author's childhood experiences when his family moved to California from Tlaquepaque, Mexico.

Our House: Stories of Levittown by Pam Conrad

Children growing up in Levittown talk about being raised in the American suburb from 1940 to the 1990s.

Fiction

Holes by Louis Sacher

Stanley Yelnats has come to Camp Green Lake in Texas and is forced to dig holes every day. Stanley stumbles across a mystery, and the action begins in this 1999 Newbery Medal Book.

Francie by Karen English

Francie is a young African-American girl growing up in the 1930s in Alabama, who tutors a 16-year-old boy. When he is falsely accused, Francie comes to his defense, in this 2000 Coretta Scott King Award Honor Book.

UNIT 4
Passages

"A journey of a thousand miles must begin with a single step."

—Lao-Tzu
(Chinese philosopher, ca. 604–531 B.C.E.)

Discuss the Theme

Passages

Doing new things can be exciting. Sometimes it can be a little scary. But change can take you in different directions and lead to new adventures and experiences. In this unit, you will read "Flowers," a poem about how a young girl feels after singing her first solo (a song sung by one person alone). In "Gilda," you will read about Alma. You will learn how this new student's experience at school turned out better than she thought it would. You will see how a new friendship leads two children to make a change that will affect both their lives in "The Secret Garden." In "My Season with Penguins," you will find out about a woman and her trip to the Antarctic to paint and study penguins.

- What new things have you tried lately?
- What big changes have you made in your life?
- Is it easy or hard to try new things? Why?
- What new things would you like to do in the future?

WRITING FOCUS:
Response to Literature

13

Before You Read

a poem by Eloise Greenfield

Background

Did you ever sing, or dance, or act on a stage in front of an audience? If you did, how did you feel? In the poem "Flowers," by Eloise Greenfield, you will discover how a young girl feels about singing her first solo on stage.

LEARNING OBJECTIVES

- Understand tone and meaning in poetry
- Use correct capitalization
- Identify rhyming words
- Respond to literature through ideas and images

Building Your Vocabulary

1. Look at the words below. Match each one with the word that is most closely related to it. Write the three pairs on a sheet of paper.

   tear   flowers
   bouquet   sing
   solo   eye

2. Make up a sentence using each pair of words. Share your sentences with a partner.

Reading: Classify categories of words

Reading Strategy

Understand tone and meaning in poetry

Reading a poem is different from reading a story or an article in a newspaper or magazine. A poem usually conveys emotions rather than facts. One way a poem conveys emotions is through its tone. Tone is an attitude or feeling that a poet creates through words and images. To understand tone, readers should carefully read poems out loud to hear the poet's voice. Readers should listen for sounds and should picture the images the poet creates. All these add to the tone.

Applying the Reading Strategy

To identify tone in a poem:

1. Look for words that describe emotions, such as **happy** or **sad**. What do those words tell you about the tone of the poem?

2. Are the sentences long or short? How does sentence length contribute to the feeling of the poem?

3. Look for words that relate to sight, sound, taste, smell, or touch. What feelings do those words create?

4. Does the author repeat any words, or categories of words? If so, how does the repetition add to the feeling the poet wants to convey?

Reading: Define how tone or meaning is conveyed in poetry; Reading: Extract appropriate and significant information from the text

Flowers

a poem by Eloise Greenfield

My stepfather brought me flowers today.
For my first solo—my first bouquet,
yellow and peach and purple and red,
"Daughter, you sang like an angel," he said.
My stepfather brought me flowers, and I
pretended there wasn't a tear in his eye,
flowers and happiness tied with a bow,
because I had just sung my first solo.

As You Read

1. What words does the poet use to describe feelings?

2. What words does the poet use that relate to sight? To sound?

3. What words or phrases does the poet repeat?

4. What kind of punctuation does the poet use? Are the sentences long or short?

stepfather: the husband of one's mother and not one's father

About the Author

Eloise Greenfield

Eloise Greenfield lives in Washington, D.C. and is the author of many books for children. In 1997 she received the Award for Excellence in Poetry for Children from the National Council of Teachers of English. Ms. Greenfield often works with the illustrator Jan Spivey Gilchrist. The poem "Flowers" comes from the book *Angels*, which they created as a team.

Reading: Define how tone or meaning is conveyed in poetry

Retell It!

Retell the poem you just read as a story. Include important details. Write down your story and put it in your portfolio.

Think, Discuss, Write

Discuss these questions in small groups. Then write your answers on a separate sheet of paper.

1. **Structure** Poets can choose to write in **verse** (using words that rhyme, such as **flower** and **shower**). They can also use **free verse**, using words that do not rhyme at the end of lines. Is "Flowers" written in verse or free verse?

2. **Structure** What punctuation does the author use?

3. **Tone** Are the sentences in the poem long or short? How does the length of each sentence affect the tone?

4. **Compare** Why does the stepfather compare the girl's voice to an angel's voice?

5. **Make inferences** Why does the stepfather in the poem cry?

6. **Make inferences** Whose feelings do we find out about in this poem?

7. **Cause and effect** How does the tone of the poem help us share those feelings?

What's Your Opinion?

Look at the following ways you can learn about people's feelings and ideas.

1. Short story
2. Poem
3. Magazine or newspaper article
4. Movie or TV program
5. Conversation

Which do you like best? Which do you like least? On a separate sheet of paper, draw a chart like the one to the right. Write the number of each item in order, from most to least.

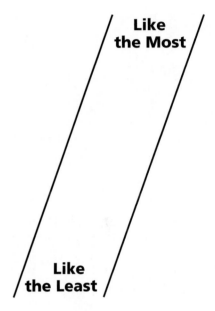

Like the Most

Like the Least

Launch into Grammar

Capitalization   Capital letters should be used (1) at the beginning of a sentence, (2) for proper nouns and the pronoun I, (3) for names and titles, and (4) for abbreviations.

Work with a partner to find the capitalization missing in the sentences below. Rewrite each corrected sentence on a separate sheet of paper.

1. the concert began at two o'clock on wednesday.

2. when i saw my stepfather, i smiled.

3. first, rodney and darla sang a duet by mozart.

4. every seat at jefferson junior high school was filled.

5. in the audience i saw mayor wiggins and dr. mary lasky.

Written conventions: Use correct capitalization

 For more practice with capitalization, complete page 99 of the Student Workbook.

Launch into Word Analysis

Rhyming words   Two words that end in the same sound or sounds are said to **rhyme**. Here are some examples of rhyming words. Word endings don't need to be spelled the same to rhyme.

red - bed	hot - pot	bite - right
play - weigh	stuff - tough	blue - threw

With a partner, find each pair of rhyming words in the poem "Flowers." Then work together to find a word that rhymes with each of the following words. Write the word pairs you find on a separate sheet of paper.

ring	pan	cat
cheese	break	chair
nice	wood	kiss

 For more practice with rhyming words, complete page 100 of the Student Workbook.

Launch into Writing

Interpret a poem   Read the poem on page 169 carefully. Pay attention to every word as you read. Try to connect the situation described in the poem to your own experiences and your own knowledge of the world.

Study Tip

As you read, take note of words that are capitalized. Can you figure out which rule on page 167 applies?

Reading: Create and state a series of rhyming words

The Apple Cats

I came to my sister's soccer game.
The Apple Cats is her team's name.
I watched them race up and down the field.
They kicked the ball — the audience squealed.
"Goal!" the fans sitting next to us cried.
Which team scored? The other side.
The game soon ended — I cheered loud.
The Apple Cats lost, but I'm still proud.

Work together with a partner to interpret "The Apple Cats." What does the poem mean to you?

 For more practice with interpreting complete poems, complete pages 102–103 of the Student Workbook.

Writing Tip

Before you start to write, relax. Then, write down as many words as you can about your topic. This is called **brainstorming**. This will help you think of words about your subject before you write.

Writing: Write responses to literature: Organize the interpretation around several clear ideas, premises, or images

14

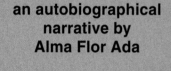

an autobiographical
narrative by
Alma Flor Ada

Before You Read

Background

Have you ever changed schools or moved to a new city? How did you feel about the change? In this autobiography, Cuban-born Alma Flor Ada tells how she felt about changing schools in the middle of fourth grade. Read on to see how her ballet teacher, Gilda, changed her life.

LEARNING OBJECTIVES

- Connect main ideas to other sources and topics
- Create and punctuate compound-complex sentences
- Recognize and use words from other languages
- Respond to literature by using examples and facts from a text to support your ideas

Building Your Vocabulary

1. Alma Flor Ada talks a lot about her learning experiences in "Gilda." Some of her experiences were in grade school, and some were in ballet school. Look at the vocabulary on page 171. On a separate sheet of paper, list the words in the correct category, following the example.

Reading: Interpret information from diagrams and charts

imperative	first grade
grace	board
conjunction	positions
waltz	leotards
preposition	slippers

Grade School	Ballet School
imperative	*grace*

2. Check your responses with a partner. Can you add any more items to the lists?

Reading Strategy

Connect main ideas to other sources and topics

As you read, you should try to connect main ideas in the story to things you know or are familiar with. For example, when you read about Cuba, you should try to connect what you read to what you know about Cuba. This can help you get a better idea of what the story is about.

Applying the Reading Strategy

1. As you read the narrative, find the main idea of each paragraph. Have you read any books or magazines that are linked to this main idea? Have you seen any movies or TV shows that are related to the topic?

2. Use any connection you make to better understand what you are reading. For example, the story you are about to read

takes place in Cuba. Do you know where Cuba is located on a map? Do you know what language people speak there?

3. Try using the connections you were able to make. For example, after you finish the story, you might go to a Web site about Cuba. If possible, link one source to additional sources to find out even more information.

Reading: Connect main ideas by identifying their relationships to other sources

Gilda

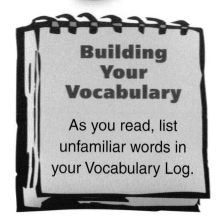

an autobiographical narrative by Alma Flor Ada

When midway through the school year my fourth-grade teacher, Gladys Carnero, moved to Havana, I felt lost. Then I became sick. First I caught one cold after another, then the measles, and finally the mumps. My wonderful parents realized that something lay beneath this. The *Colegio Episcopal* which I had been attending was unbearable to me if Gladys Carnero was no longer there. So, my parents transferred me to a new school.

Although it might have been a relief at the beginning of the school year, this transfer became another kind of nightmare. I arrived as the new child in the middle of the year—to a class where all of the other children had known each other since first grade. To make it worse, at the new school, *Colegio El Porvenir,* the students were seated according to their academic performance. Those with the best grades sat in the front; those with bad grades sat in back. Since I had no grades yet, they sat me at the very back.

In the last row, I was surrounded mostly by boys who were the tallest in the class. I, a year younger than my classmates, was the shortest. Furthermore, no one had discovered yet that I needed glasses. I could not see anything on the board.

I tried to hide behind one of the students who sat in front of me, but it seemed that my strategy only brought me harder questions

Reading: Connect main ideas by identifying their relationships to other sources

from the teacher. "Indicative," "subjunctive," and "imperative," sounded equally horrible to me. I loved words like "zephyr" and "zenith," "nectar" and "ambrosia," "friendship" and "loyalty." But the words "preposition," "conjunction," and "subordinate" sounded almost as ugly as "sulfur" and "hate" to me.

Because my parents had been so understanding, I felt I could not tell them how unhappy I was. There was only one thing that allowed me to survive that horrible school with its treeless cement yard—a school without songs, without drawing, without stories, without friends.

On my way to school one day, a couple of blocks down a side street that I had followed just to delay my arrival, an unexpected wisp of music greeted me, merrily escaping from a tall window behind a carved wooden railing.

On tiptoes, grasping the wooden railing, I peered inside the old colonial house from which the waltz spilled onto the street.

Inside, an enormous mirror reflected a dozen young girls, in pink leotards and black slippers, practicing at the barre. At the piano an older woman played the unending waltz. In front of the class, holding a tall staff, stood a young blond woman, so pale she was almost translucent. She had incredible eyes—eyes that took in everything: the girls, the piano

zephyr: a gentle breeze
zenith: the highest point
ambrosia: something extremely pleasing to eat
barre: handrail used by ballet dancers

As You Read

1. What does the narrator hear one day that surprises her? Where was it coming from?

2. What does she see when she looks into the window of the old house?

3. From the context of the story, what do you think the word *translucent* means?

Reading: Connect main ideas by identifying their relationships to other sources

player, and indeed the whole room, including the far corner where a group of elegant ladies sat in mahogany rocking chairs, sleepily cooling themselves with silk fans.

As the days went by, school became bearable only because as soon as the long-awaited bell rang, I would run and cling to the window of the ballet school, imagining myself in soft slippers, changing positions, second, third, fourth, performing a *jeté* or a *plié*.

One afternoon, the pale teacher disappeared from view, and before I realized what was happening, she was standing on the sidewalk by my side. "Do you want to study ballet? What is your name?"

Her voice was as soft as her gaze. "Come in," she said. "Come in."

Once she knew who I was, she called my mother and offered to accept me in her class. My life was changed, not only after school, but in school, too!

I was never again bothered by prepositions and conjunctions, nor by my inability to remember how much is seven times eight. Nor did I mind anymore sitting in the back of the class, although slowly, without really noticing how, I managed to move to the middle rows and even to the front.

I lived only for the moment when the bell rang and I could run to the ballet school. And it wasn't that I did very well there. I did not. I was placed at the end of the line, and there I

mahogany: reddish-brown wood from a West Indian tree

Social Studies

Did you know that Cubans are one of the three largest groups of Spanish speakers living in the United States today? Many Cubans live in Florida, especially Miami, along the East Coast, and in New York City. The Cuban section of Miami is called "Little Havana" because there are so many Cubans living there. (Havana is the capital of Cuba.)

Reading: Connect main ideas by identifying their relationships to other sources

stayed for as long as my classes continued. In spite of my love for music and for the beauty of the movements, it was as if I had three feet, or as though my left and right sides had traded places. But in spite of my clumsy attempts, so devoid of grace, how wonderful it was to be there!

No matter what mistake I made, I was never criticized nor ridiculed by Gilda, the teacher. Although I saw her become impatient once in a while, it was only when someone who could naturally do better was not paying attention. To me she offered the same gentleness she showed the youngest of the girls, looking at me with a sweet look of complicity, as if to say "You know that I know you cannot dance, but that you long to be here, and I welcome you."

I was very surprised when one day my teacher invited me to stay after class. That was the beginning of a beautiful friendship that was cherished equally by both of us.

As You Read

1. Does the narrator do well in ballet school? How do you know?

2. Find the words in the selection that tell you the narrator's reactions to ballet.

complicity: participation in a secret activity

About the Author

Alma Flor Ada

Alma Flor Ada lives in San Francisco and is a professor of multicultural education at the University of San Francisco. She was born in Camagüey, Cuba, and has also lived in Spain and Peru. She has published books in the United States, Spain, Mexico, and Peru. She travels around the United States speaking on topics such as multiculturalism and education.

Reading: Connect main ideas by identifying their relationships to other sources

After You Read

Retell It!

What do you think Gilda was like in general? What did she think of teaching? What did she think of her students? With a partner, retell the story from Gilda's point of view.

Think, Discuss, Write

With a partner, discuss your answers to these questions. Then write them down.

1. **Structure**   Is the selection you just read nonfiction or fiction—that is, did it really happen or not? How do you know?

2. **Recall details**   List three facts that the narrator gives us. What are her feelings about each fact?

3. **Making inferences**   Did the narrator like to answer questions in class? How do you know?

4. **Recall details**   Did the narrator tell her parents how she felt?

5. **Tone**   Write down details from the selection that tell you how the narrator felt about ballet.

6. **Recall details**   What did the teacher look like?

7. **Cause and effect**   How did going to ballet school change the narrator's performance in grade school?

What's Your Opinion?

Work with a partner. Decide on a new experience that you have both had recently. Have you both moved to a new home or apartment? Have you

Reading: Distinguish facts, supported inferences, and opinions in text

had a new teacher? Copy the chart and write down your own experience. Write positive things about your experience under "Positive." Write down any negative things under "Negative."

Experience: *Starting in a new school*

Positive	Negative
new friends, new teachers	*being the new person, not knowing anyone*

Now answer the questions below.

1. How is your experience similar to the narrator's experience in the story "Gilda"?

2. Did you share some of the same feelings? If so, which ones?

Launch into Grammar

Compound-complex sentences   Compound-complex sentences have two or more clauses that can stand on their own as sentences (independent clauses) and a dependent clause that cannot stand on its own. Use a conjunction to join one independent clause with the other independent and dependent clause—*and, but, or, yet, for, so.*

> **independent clause:** "One afternoon, the pale teacher disappeared from view,
> **conjunction:** and
> **dependent clause:** before I realized what was happening,
> **independent clause:** she was standing on the sidewalk by my side."

Work with a partner. Find another compound-complex sentence in the reading.

Written conventions: Use compound-complex sentences

For more practice with compound-complex sentences, complete page 107 of the Student Workbook.

Launch into Word Analysis

Words from other languages English has borrowed a large number of words from other languages. Spanish words used in English include *tortilla*, *mesa*, *plaza*, and *enchilada*. What do all of the words borrowed from Spanish have in common?

Find some ballet terms in "Gilda" that come from the French. What do these words have in common? Discuss with a partner and report your answers to the class.

 For more practice with words from other languages, complete page 108 of the Student Workbook.

Launch into Writing

Support a response to literature with details
Your response to reading literature can be wide-ranging. Some pieces that you read can be deeply moving. Other pieces may barely make an impression on you. Write a paragraph that tells your reaction to the selection. Did you like it? Did it make an impression on you? Would you recommend it to others? Tell why. What details from the selection can you use to support your view?

Reading: Apply knowledge of word origins to determine the meaning of words

Here is an example.

"Gilda" really made sense to me. It's not that I am a dancer. In fact, I'm a terrible dancer. I have two left feet! When it comes to basketball, things are different. One day I saw some kids in the gym playing basketball. I said to myself, "Rita, you can do that." I was afraid, but I asked if I could play. The kids said, "Sure." To make a long story short, I am now a basketball player on the school team. Alma Flor Ada's story was important to me because it reminded me of all I had to do to become a basketball player. It's a great story!

Writing Tip

Check your paragraph. Make sure all of your sentences are complete sentences.

For more practice using supporting details, complete pages 110–111 of the Student Workbook.

Writing: Write responses to literature: Support judgments through references to the text and prior knowledge

The Secret Garden

an excerpt from a novel by Frances Hodgson Burnett

Background

The main character in *The Secret Garden,* Mary Lennox, has had some difficult and sad experiences. Mary has been sent to England to Misselthwaite, the large, dark, and frightening house with a mysterious secret garden where her uncle, Mr. Craven, and his housekeeper, Mrs. Medlock, live. Mary decides to look for the source of a mysterious noise she has been hearing at night.

LEARNING OBJECTIVES

- Visualize the context or setting of a story
- Create compound sentences and punctuate them correctly
- Understand shades of meaning between words
- Organize information

Building Your Vocabulary

Read the sentences below and on the top of page 181. With a partner, discuss the meaning of the words underlined.

"Perhaps the fact that she was in a <u>rebellious</u> mood made her <u>bold</u>."

Reading: Monitor expository text for unknown words or words with novel meanings by using word, sentence, and paragraph clues to determine meaning

"She thought she remembered the corners she must turn to find the short corridor with the door covered with <u>tapestry</u> . . ."

"Down this <u>passage</u> and then to the left, and then up two broad steps, and then to the right again."

". . . and a night-light burning by the side of a carved, four-poster bed hung with <u>brocade</u> . . ."

Reading Strategy

Visualize the context or setting of a story

In many stories, especially those that contain mystery or suspense, writers often use descriptive words to help the reader see the same sights and feel the same emotions as the characters.

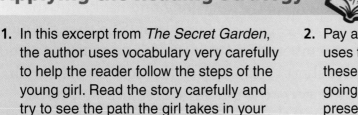

Applying the Reading Strategy

1. In this excerpt from *The Secret Garden*, the author uses vocabulary very carefully to help the reader follow the steps of the young girl. Read the story carefully and try to see the path the girl takes in your mind. Try to imagine what each place and person looks like. Which words help you see this? How do you feel as you follow her journey through the house?

2. Pay attention to the words the author uses to describe each scene. How do these words help you visualize what's going on, and what kind of mood is present in the story?

3. Try removing some of the adjectives and adverbs that helped you visualize a scene in the story. How does the mood change?

Reading: Analyze the influence of setting on the problem and its resolution

The Secret Garden

an excerpt from a novel by Frances Hodgson Burnett

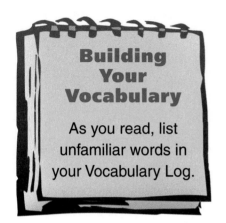

Building Your Vocabulary

As you read, list unfamiliar words in your Vocabulary Log.

She had been lying awake, turning from side to side for about an hour, when suddenly something made her sit up in bed and turn her head towards the door listening. She listened and she listened.

"It isn't the wind now," she said in a loud whisper. "That isn't the wind. It is different. It is that crying I heard before."

The door of her room was ajar and the sound came down the corridor, a far-off sound of fretful crying. She listened for a few minutes and each minute she became more and more sure. She felt as if she must find out what it was. It seemed even stranger than the secret garden and the buried key. Perhaps the fact that she was in a rebellious mood made her bold. She put her foot out of bed and stood on the floor.

"I am going to find out what it is," she said. "Everybody is in bed and I don't care about Mrs. Medlock—I don't care!"

There was a candle by her side and she took it up and went softly out of the room. The corridor looked very long and dark, but she was too excited to mind that. She thought she remembered the corners she must turn to find the short corridor with the door covered with tapestry—the one Mrs. Medlock had come through the day she lost herself. The sound had come up that passage. So she went on

ajar: slightly open
fretful: complaining and irritable
passage: a corridor or path

As You Read

1. When does Mary hear the sound?
2. What does the strange noise sound like?

Reading: Analyze the influence of setting on the problem and its resolution

with her dim light, almost feeling her way, her heart beating so loud that she fancied she could hear it. The far-off, faint crying went on and led her. Sometimes it stopped for a moment or so and then began again. Was this the right corner to turn? She stopped and thought. Yes, it was. Down this passage and then to the left, and then up two broad steps, and then to the right again. Yes, there was the tapestry door.

She pushed it open very gently and closed it behind her, and she stood in the corridor and could hear the crying quite plainly, though it was not loud. It was on the other side of the wall at her left and a few yards farther on there was a door. She could see a glimmer of light coming from beneath it. The Someone was crying in that room, and it was quite a young Someone.

So she walked to the door and pushed it open, and there she was standing in the room!

It was a big room with ancient, handsome furniture in it. There was a low fire glowing faintly on the hearth and a night-light burning by the side of a carved, four-poster bed hung with brocade, and on the bed was lying a boy, crying pitifully.

Mary wondered if she was in a real place or if she had fallen asleep again and was dreaming without knowing it.

The boy had a sharp, delicate face, the colour of ivory, and he seemed to have eyes too big for

brocade: a rich fabric with raised patterns

The Secret Garden 183

it. He had also a lot of hair which tumbled over his forehead in heavy locks and made his thin face seem smaller. He looked like a boy who had been ill, but he was crying more as if he were tired and cross than as if he were in pain.

Mary stood near the door with her candle in her hand, holding her breath. Then she crept across the room, and as she drew nearer the light attracted the boy's attention and he turned his head on his pillow and stared at her, his grey eyes opening so wide that they seemed immense.

"Who are you?" he said at last in a half-frightened whisper. "Are you a ghost?"

"No, I am not," Mary answered, her own whisper sounding half-frightened. "Are you one?"

He stared and stared. Mary could not help noticing what strange eyes he had. They were agate-grey and they looked too big for his face because they had black lashes all round them.

"No," he replied, after waiting a moment or so. "I am Colin."

"Who is Colin?" she faltered.

"I am Colin Craven. Who are you?"

"I am Mary Lennox. Mr. Craven is my uncle."

"He is my father," said the boy.

"Your father!" gasped Mary. "No one ever told me he had a boy! Why didn't they?"

"Come here," he said, still keeping his strange eyes fixed on her with an anxious expression.

cross: angry
agate-grey: a certain shade of grey

Reading: Analyze the influence of setting on the problem and its resolution

She came close to the bed and he put out his hand and touched her.

"You are real, aren't you?" he said. "I have such real dreams very often. You might be one of them."

Mary had slipped on a woollen wrapper before she left her room and she put a piece of it between his fingers.

"Rub that and see how thick and warm it is," she said. "I will pinch you a little if you like, to show you how real I am. For a minute I thought you might be a dream too."

"Where did you come from?" he asked.

"From my own room. The wind wuthered so I couldn't go to sleep and I heard someone crying and wanted to find out who it was. What were you crying for?"

"Because I couldn't go to sleep either, and my head ached. Tell me your name again."

"Mary Lennox. Did no one ever tell you I had come to live here?"

He was still fingering the fold of her wrapper, but he began to look a little more as if he believed in her reality.

"No," he answered. "They daren't. "

"Why?" asked Mary.

"Because I should have been afraid you would see me. I won't let people see me and talk me over."

wrapper: a shawl
wuthered: blew with a roaring sound
daren't: wouldn't dare
talk me over: talk about me

As You Read

1. Who is Colin Craven?
2. How does Mary prove to Colin she is real?

Reading: Analyze the influence of setting on the problem and its resolution

"Why?" Mary asked again, feeling ever more mystified.

"Because I am like this always, ill and having to lie down. My father won't let people talk me over, either. The servants are not allowed to speak about me. If I live I may be a <mark>hunchback,</mark> but I shan't live. My father hates to think I may be like him."

"Oh, what a queer house this is!" Mary exclaimed. "What a queer house! Everything is a kind of secret. Rooms are locked up and gardens are locked up—and you! Have you been locked up?"

"No. I stay in this room because I don't want to be moved out of it. It tires me too much."

"Does your father come and see you?" Mary ventured.

"Sometimes. Generally when I am asleep. He doesn't want to see me."

"Why?" Mary could not help asking again.

A sort of angry shadow passed over the boy's face.

"My mother died when I was born and it makes him <mark>wretched</mark> to look at me. He thinks I don't know, but I've heard people talking. He almost hates me."

"He hates the garden, because she died," said Mary, half speaking to herself.

"What garden?" the boy asked.

"Oh! Just—just a garden she used to like," Mary stammered. "Have you been here always?"

hunchback: a person with a humped back
wretched: sad, depressed

As You Read

1. Why does Mary think this is such a strange house?
2. Why does Colin say his father hates him?

Reading: Analyze the influence of setting on the problem and its resolution

"Nearly always. Sometimes I have been taken to places at the seaside, but I won't stay because people stare at me. I used to wear an iron thing to keep my back straight, but a grand doctor came from London to see me and said it was stupid. He told them to take it off and keep me out in the fresh air. I hate fresh air and I don't want to go out."

"I didn't when first I came here," said Mary. "Why do you keep looking at me like that?"

"Because of the dreams that are so real," he answered rather fretfully. "Sometimes when I open my eyes I don't believe I'm awake."

"We're both awake," said Mary. She glanced round the room with its high ceiling and shadowy corners and dim firelight. "It looks quite like a dream, and it's the middle of the night, and everybody in the house is asleep— everybody but us."

"I don't want it to be a dream," the boy said restlessly.

Mary thought of something all at once.

"If you don't like people to see you," she began, "do you want me to go away?"

He still held the fold of her wrapper and he gave it a little pull.

"No," he said. "I should be sure you were a dream if you went. If you are real, sit down on that big footstool and talk. I want to hear about you."

Mary put down her candle on the table near the bed and sat down on the cushioned stool.

grand: distinguished, important

should be sure: would be convinced

Reading: Analyze the influence of setting on the problem and its resolution

She did not want to go away at all. She wanted to stay in the mysterious, hidden-away room and talk to the mysterious boy.

"What do you want me to tell you?" she said.

He wanted to know how long she had been at Misselthwaite; he wanted to know which corridor her room was on; he wanted to know what she had been doing; if she disliked the moor as he disliked it; where she had lived before she came to Yorkshire. She answered all these questions and many more, and he lay back on his pillow and listened. He made her tell him a great deal about India and about her voyage across the ocean. She found out that because he had been an invalid he had not learned things as other children had. One of his nurses had taught him to read when he was quite little and he was always reading and looking at pictures in splendid books.

Though his father rarely saw him when he was awake, he was given all sorts of wonderful things to amuse himself with. He never seemed to have been amused, however. He could have anything he asked for and was never made to do anything he did not like to do.

"Everyone is obliged to do what pleases me," he said indifferently. "It makes me ill to be angry. No one believes I shall live to grow up."

He said it as if he was so accustomed to the idea that it had ceased to matter to him at all. He seemed to like the sound of Mary's voice.

moor: open hilly land
invalid: someone who is sick
obliged: required

Reading: Analyze the influence of setting on the problem and its resolution

As she went on talking he listened in a drowsy, interested way. Once or twice she wondered if he were not gradually falling into a doze. But at last he asked a question which opened up a new subject.

"How old are you?" he asked.

"I am ten," answered Mary, forgetting herself for the moment, "and so are you."

"How do you know that?" he demanded in a surprised voice.

"Because when you were born, the garden door was locked and the key was buried. And it has been locked for ten years."

Colin half sat up, turning towards her, leaning on his elbows.

"What garden door was locked? Who did it? Where was the key buried?" he exclaimed, as if he were suddenly very much interested.

"It—it was the garden Mr. Craven hates," said Mary nervously. "He locked the door. No one—no one knew where he buried the key."

"What sort of a garden is it?" Colin persisted eagerly.

"No one has been allowed to go into it for ten years," was Mary's careful answer.

But it was too late to be careful. He was too much like herself. He, too, had had nothing to think about, and the idea of a hidden garden attracted him as it had attracted her. He asked question after question. Where was it? Had she never looked for the door? Had she never asked the gardeners?

As You Read

1. How old is Mary?
2. Why has Colin never been in the garden?

The Secret Garden 189

"They won't talk about it," said Mary. "I think they have been told not to answer questions."

"I would make them," said Colin defiantly.

"Could you?" Mary faltered, beginning to feel frightened. If he could make people answer questions, who knew what might happen?

"Everyone is obliged to please me. I told you that," he said. "If I were to live, this place would some time belong to me. They all know that. I would make them tell me."

Mary had not known that she herself had been spoiled, but she could see quite plainly that this mysterious boy had been. He thought that the whole world belonged to him. How peculiar he was and how coolly he spoke of not living.

"Do you think you won't live?" she asked, partly because she was curious and partly in hope of making him forget the garden.

"I don't suppose I shall," he answered as indifferently as he had spoken before. "Ever since I remember anything I have heard people say I shan't. At first they thought I was too little to understand, and now they think I don't hear. But I do. My doctor is my father's cousin. He is quite poor and if I die he will have all Misselthwaite when my father is dead. I should think he wouldn't want me to live."

defiantly: rebelliously
shan't: shall not or won't

Reading: Analyze the influence of setting on the problem and its resolution

"Do you want to live?" inquired Mary.

"No," he answered, in a cross, tired fashion. "But I don't want to die. When I feel ill, I lie here and think about it until I cry and cry."

"I have heard you crying three times," Mary said, "but I did not know who it was. Were you crying about that?" She did so want him to forget the garden.

"I dare say," he answered. "Let us talk about something else. Talk about that garden. Don't you want to see it?"

"Yes," answered Mary in quite a low voice.

"I do," he went on persistently. "I don't think I ever really wanted to see anything before, but I want to see that garden. I want the key dug up. I want the door unlocked. I would let them take me there in my chair. That would be getting fresh air. I am going to make them open the door."

As You Read

1. Why is Colin so strange to Mary?
2. Do you think Colin really wants to die?

About the Author

Frances Hodgson Burnett

Frances Hodgson Burnett was a novelist born in Manchester, England, in 1849. When she was 16 years old, she came to the United States, where she lived until her death in 1924. She is the author of several well-known children's books, including *Little Lord Fauntleroy* and *The Secret Garden*, which she considered to be her best novel.

After You Read

Retell It!

With a partner, retell the story from Colin's or Mr. Craven's point of view. Note how the story changes from someone else's point of view.

Think, Discuss, Write

In small groups, discuss the following questions.

1. **Tone**   How does the tone of this story shift from the beginning to the end?

2. **Cause and effect**   Do you think that Mary and Colin will each benefit from knowing each other?

3. **Character**   Describe what Colin looks like.

4. **Make inferences**   Why does Colin think his father doesn't like him?

5. **Recall details**   What are two of the questions that Colin asks Mary?

6. **Compare and contrast**   How are Mary and Colin alike? How are they different?

What's Your Opinion?

Answer the following questions, then fill in a chart like the one shown on page 193.

1. What did you think about Mary? Did you like her or admire her? Why or why not?

2. What did you think about Colin? Did you like him or admire him? Why or why not?

3. Based on what the other characters say about Mr. Craven, what do you think of him? Do you like or admire him? Why or why not?

Reading: Restate facts and details in the text to clarify and organize ideas

4. Copy the chart onto a separate sheet of paper. Fill in the chart with words to describe Mary, Colin, and Mr. Craven. Try to use a total of at least five words from the story.

Mary	Colin	Mr. Craven
curious	*ill*	*sad*

Launch into Grammar

Compound sentences   Compound sentences have two or more clauses that can stand on their own as sentences. The subject of each clause must agree with the verb.

> **Example:**   Colin rings the bell, and the servants come to him.

> **First clause**—Subject: Colin   Verb: rings
> **Second clause**—Subject: servants   Verb: come

With a partner, choose the correct verbs to complete each sentence. Write your answers on a separate sheet of paper.

1. Mary (hear, hears) noises, but they (is, are) coming from a hidden room.

2. Colin's doctors (want, wants) him to stay in bed, but Colin (have, has) plans to go out.

3. Mary and Colin (is, are) now friends, and Colin (is, are) no longer lonely.

The Secret Garden   193

Extend: Look at an E-mail, letter, or report you have written. Do you usually write simple sentences, compound sentences, or both? Try using different kinds of sentences for variety.

 For more practice with compound sentences, complete page 115 of the Student Workbook.

Launch into Word Analysis

Words with similar meaning Sometimes writers use words or phrases that are similar in meaning, instead of repeating the same word over and over. This increases readers' vocabulary.

Examples: The **corridor** looked very long and dark. The sound had come up that **passage**.

Write the words below on a separate sheet of paper. Match each word on the left with the word on the right that is closest in meaning. Then find where the words are used in the story.

invalid	candle
far-off	indifferently
dim light	ill
coolly	faint

 For more practice with words with similar meaning, complete page 117 of the Student Workbook.

Study Tip

You can usually guess the meaning of a word from **context** (the other words and sentences around a word). Sometimes you may need a dictionary to figure out the difference between two words whose meanings are very similar. Look up the definitions for **cross** and **fretful**, for example, and you will see that the two words are almost **synonyms** (two words that mean about the same thing).

Reading: Understand and explain "shades of meaning" in related words

Launch into Writing

Organize information   When you list information in your writing, there are a number of ways to organize the items on your list. You can organize by category. You can organize by how large or small things are. You can organize by time, position, color, height, weight, importance, price, number or amount, or age. You can choose some special quality, such as hardness, softness, brightness, or speed, as your organizing principle. In general, think of the feature or quality that you want to highlight, and organize according to that feature or quality. Here are some examples:

Organize by **size**:   elephant, giraffe, bear, tiger, dog, mouse

Organize by **speed**: tiger, dog, bear, elephant, giraffe, mouse

Organize by **height**: giraffe, elephant, bear, tiger, dog, mouse

   With a partner, organize these items: sports car, minivan, tricycle, truck, motorcycle, train, bicycle.

Organize by **size**: _____

Organize by **weight**: _____

Organize by **fuel burned**: _____

Organize by **speed**: _____

 For more practice with organizing information, complete page 118–119 of the Student Workbook.

Writing Tip

When you react to literature, you form an opinion. To form an opinion, you should find examples in the literature to support that opinion. To give an opinion, use phrases like *I think, It seems to me, It is my opinion that,* and *I believe.* To support the opinion, use phrases like *the author states, the character says, to quote the text,* and *we are told in the reading.*

Writing: Use a variety of organizational patterns, including comparison and contrast, categories, spatial order, or order of importance

16

Before You Read

Background

This selection is the personal account of a woman named Sophie Webb. Sophie set off on an expedition to Antarctica to study and sketch penguins. The trip to Antarctica was a great change from her life in San Francisco, California.

My Season with PENGUINS

an excerpt from a nonfiction book by Sophie Webb

Building Your Vocabulary

1. Look at the word cluster at the top of page 197. Come up with a category that fits each group of words.

2. With a partner, discuss the words. Can you think of other words that fit the categories?

Reading: Demonstrate knowledge of specificity among grade-appropriate words

Cluster Map

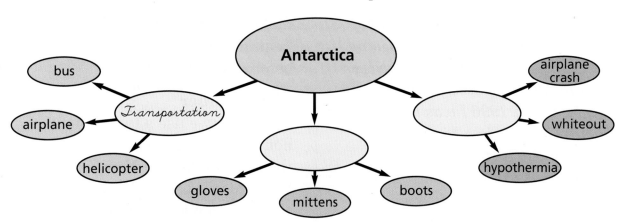

Reading Strategy

Identify point of view   In a story or an article, the speaker is called the *narrator*. There are two common points of view for the narrator of a story. A **first-person** narrator tells the story from the "I" point of view. A **third-person** narrator tells the story from the outside, or "he" and "she" point of view.

Applying the Reading Strategy

1. Look at the story from the beginning. Does the narrator refer to him- or herself as *I* or *me*? What kind of narrator does this story have?

2. A first-person narrator can be an important character in the story. He or she can get closer to the action and more personally involved in the story than a third-person narrator. You, the reader, view events through the first-person narrator's eyes only. Whatever the narrator *doesn't* see, you don't see either. What is something that Sophie Webb can't see but you want to know about?

3. A third-person narrator is not as close to the story as a first-person narrator. He or she often knows more than a first-person narrator. In a third-person story, you witness events through the eyes of the main characters. You see how *they* feel, not how the narrator feels. Do you know a story told in third-person narration?

Reading: Distinguish facts, supported inferences, and opinions in text

My Season with PENGUINS

an excerpt from a nonfiction book by Sophie Webb

I've traveled in many countries painting, drawing, and studying birds. For years I dreamed of going to Antarctica to see penguins. Never did I think this would become a reality, but in 1996 I was invited by David Ainley to join his project studying Adélie penguins in the Antarctic. It was an opportunity to live with penguins for two months during the Antarctic summer. I jumped at the chance.

01 December
This is the beginning of my long journey south, and halfway around the globe. I start by taking a bus from my home to the airport in San Francisco, where I meet the rest of the U.S. contingent of our research group: David, Grant, Ian, Sacha,

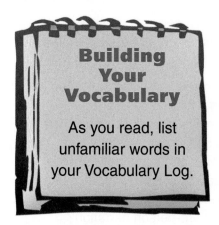

Building Your Vocabulary

As you read, list unfamiliar words in your Vocabulary Log.

Adélie penguins: small Antarctic penguins

and Sue. We board the plane and make the eleven-hour flight to New Zealand, the last stop in civilization before the Antarctic.

03 December
It's 07:30 (we use a twenty-four-hour clock) and there's land below, the North Island of New Zealand. We land in Auckland, where it is cloudy and warm—summer weather. We're in the Southern Hemisphere now, where the seasons are reversed from back home in California.

We get our baggage: six large boxes filled with computers and other scientific equipment and several bags with our personal gear.

04 December
Our flight to McMurdo, Antarctica, is delayed for a day due to poor weather.

05 December
We get to the Clothing Distribution Center by 06:00 and change into our warm clothing, put on our dog tags, check in, have breakfast, and wait. Finally, we're loaded onto

dog tags: identification necklaces

Reading: Distinguish facts, supported inferences, and opinions in text

a bus. We make our way to the runway, where a New Zealand Royal Air Force plane awaits us. It's a military cargo carrier, low-slung and pot-bellied with four turbo engines, two per side. We're ushered from the bus to one side of the pavement to wait while the plane is being loaded.

After a half-hour we are allowed to board the plane. The "seats" made of red webbing are really not much more than benches flanking each side of the plane. I sit at the end of a bench. Next to me there is a huge stack of boxes containing lettuce and eggs strapped to the floor. The engines finally start, and the plane begins shimmying down the runway. There are only a few sparsely placed portholes on each side, so I feel, rather than watch, the takeoff. After fifteen minutes the engines stop their straining and relax. I look around and everyone I see is either reading or napping. Conversation is impossible due to the engine noise, and everyone is wearing earplugs.

06 December

Up early after a restless sleep. It will take a while for me to get used to the twenty-four-hour daylight.

As You Read

1. How long will the author spend living with the penguins?

2. What season is it in New Zealand when the author lands?

cargo: items carried by a ship, airplane or truck

shimmying: shaking

Reading: Distinguish facts, supported inferences, and opinions in text

We eat breakfast, then go to a waste management meeting. Just about everything in McMurdo gets recycled or reused because it's so difficult to get resupplied and to dispose of trash. Later we meet with the National Science Foundation support staff, followed by another meeting with McMurdo Operations, the center of radio communications. The people working here will be our link to McMurdo from our field camps. We will report to them daily by radio to let them know that all is well and to inform them when we need to send samples back to the lab or need a resupply of food or other camp goods, have an emergency— or simply want to chat.

07 December
We go to survival school to learn about some of the hazards and pleasures of camping and working in the Antarctic. A storm of high winds and blowing snow can appear suddenly and cause a complete whiteout. This means one can't see more than a few feet. It's easy to get disoriented and cold in such conditions. If not prepared with some basic survival skills people can, and do, die of hypothermia. At night we camp out on the sea ice in tents and snow caves that we built. We are fortunate that it is a relatively warm, sunny, and still evening. I have trouble sleeping again because of the bright light, and because I'm excited to be camping in the Antarctic.

12 December
The weather has been stormy, so we have been stuck at McMurdo for several days. Ian flew out earlier

Connecting to

Science

In this story, the narrator tells the time using a 24-hour clock. The 24-hour clock is just another way of telling you whether the time is before or after noon. In this system, five o'clock in the morning is written as **05:00**. Five o'clock in the afternoon is written as **17:00**. Noon is written as **12:00**, and midnight is **00:00**. The 24-hour clock is used by the military, by scientists, and by some European countries.

waste management: ways of reducing and getting rid of garbage and used items

hypothermia: dangerously low body temperature

Reading: Distinguish facts, supported inferences, and opinions in text

this morning. He'll be working with our New Zealander colleagues at Cape Bird. Now it's 11:00 and the rest of us—Sacha, David, Grant, Sue, and I—are out on the helicopter pad with all our gear, ready to fly to Cape Royds. The others are going to help Sue and me for a day or two. Soon the five of us and all the equipment are loaded into the helicopter and we are up in the air skimming over the sea ice heading north.

After a half-hour we arrive at Cape Royds. It's windy but beautiful. In one direction Mount Erebus looms over us; in another we can look down a slight incline past Shackleton's hut to the Adélie penguin colony on cliffs overlooking McMurdo Sound. The fast ice (a solid sheet of frozen ocean held fast to the land) here ends abruptly with a white edge against dark blue water. The sun comes out and everything sparkles.

As You Read

1. Whose hut is close to the Adélie penguin colony?

2. What is fast ice?

3. How does the narrator feel about her expedition?

Shackleton: Sir Ernest Shackleton, a brave Irish explorer who led an expedition in Antarctica (1914–1915)

About the Author

Sophie Webb

Sophie Webb has studied and painted all kinds of birds in all kinds of places including owls in New Mexico, mockingbirds in the Galápagos, bowerbirds in Australia, and shorebirds in Alaska. She has been drawing birds and mammals since childhood, and is a biologist as well as an artist.

Reading: Distinguish facts, supported inferences, and opinions in text

After You Read

Retell It!

Work in small groups and retell the story in the third person. "My Season with Penguins" is told in first-person narration by Sophie Webb.

Think, Discuss, Write

In your same small groups from the activity above, discuss your answers to these questions. Then write them down.

1. **Point of view**   Do you think the author's first-person narration makes the story more interesting than if it were told in third-person narration? Why?

2. **Recall details**   Give three examples of where the author gives a personal reaction to an experience.

3. **Recall details**   Does a trip to the Antarctic require much preparation? How do you know?

4. **Make inferences**   Why do you think the group is going to Antarctica in the summer?

5. **Compare and contrast**   When it is winter in California, what season is it in Antarctica? How do you know?

6. **Recall details**   Why is recycling such an important issue in McMurdo? What details from the selection show this?

Connecting to Science

Seasons are extreme at the North or South Pole. Winter is dark twenty-four hours a day, and summer is light twenty-four hours a day. This has to do with the angle of the Earth and the way the sun strikes the planet during different seasons.

Reading: Ask questions and support answers by connecting prior knowledge with information from the text

What's Your Opinion?

Would you like to visit the Antarctic? Work in small groups. Tell how you would feel about each experience.

1. Studying penguins in Antarctica.

2. An eleven-hour plane ride from the U.S. to New Zealand.

3. Camping on the sea ice in tents and snow caves.

Write a short paragraph that gives your group's results, using summary phrases like *all of us, most of us, some of us, a few of us, none of us.*

Launch into Grammar

Complex sentences   A complex sentence has one clause that can stand by itself as a sentence (independent clause), and one clause that cannot stand by itself (dependent clause). Words such as *when*, *because*, *so,* and *while* make a clause dependent.

Example: **Independent clause:** Sophie studied owls. (stands on its own)
Dependent clause: When she went to New Mexico. (cannot stand on its own)
Complex sentence: Sophie studied owls when she went to New Mexico.

Writing Tip

As you read in this class and others, look for complex sentences. Identify the independent clause and the dependent clause.

With a partner, write a complex sentence using each set of clauses from the next page.

My Season with Penguins 203

Independent clause: Antarctica is bitterly cold
Dependent clause: because it gets almost no sunlight in the winter

Independent clause: people must prepare carefully
Dependent clause: when they go to Antarctica

 For more practice with complex sentences, complete page 123 of the Student Workbook.

Launch into Word Analysis

Context clues When you come across an unfamiliar word, use clues from the **context**, the surrounding words, to guess what it means. Use the context to find the meaning of the boldfaced word in the sentence:

> Everything gets recycled in the camp because it's difficult to **dispose** of trash.

Clue 1: *Dispose* is something you do with trash.
Clue 2: *Dispose* is something that is difficult to do so everything gets recycled.
Guess: *Dispose* means to **get rid of**. (correct)

Guess a meaning for the boldfaced word below. Write it on a separate piece of paper. Show your partner your guess.

> The ice ends **abruptly** with a white edge against dark blue water.

Clue 1: *Abruptly* is how the ice ends.
Clue 2: The white stops at the blue water.

Reading: Use sentence and word context to find the meaning of unknown words

For more practice using context clues, complete page 125 of the Student Workbook.

Launch into Writing

Arguments and counterarguments   If you want to change something, you must explain your position or your argument. To present a position in your writing, you need to do two things. First, you must state your argument clearly and effectively. Second, you must address the **counterarguments** that others might have. A **counterargument** is a position that goes against your own opinion. To convince others to agree with your position, you must show that you have addressed their ideas and the questions and concerns they might have.

Write a counterargument for each of the following positions—even if you agree with the position. Work with a partner.

1. Antarctica is the last true wilderness. People should not be allowed to visit there. They will ruin the environment.

2. The United States needs energy. It should drill for oil and other resources in Antarctica.

3. There is no reason to study penguins in Antarctica. It is dangerous and a waste of money.

For more practice with counterarguments, complete pages 126–127 of the Student Workbook.

Writing Tip

When you decide what your purpose is in writing, ask yourself these questions:

1. Do I want to inform?

2. Do I want to share my feelings?

3. Do I want to describe?

Writing: Write persuasive compositions: State a clear position, support with evidence, and address reader concerns

Respond to Literature: Book Review

In Unit 4 you read various types of literature:

- Chapter 13—a poem
- Chapter 14—an autobiographical narrative
- Chapter 15—an excerpt from a novel
- Chapter 16—an excerpt from a nonfiction book

Have you ever asked a friend to tell you the name of a good book to read? Many people look at book reviews to help them decide what to read. These appear in magazines and newspapers and can even be heard on TV or radio. With a partner, you'll review two of the selections you read in Unit 4. You'll give your review aloud—as if it would be heard on a radio or TV show.

Step One: Plan Your Review

1. Choose one of the readings from Unit 4.

2. Write down your reactions to the reading selection you chose. Did you like the reading? Did you dislike it? Why? Be as specific as possible.

List details. Use a chart like the one below, writing what you liked and disliked.

Liked	Disliked
The characters were curious.	The words were different from the way I talk.
Examples: Mary wants to find out what made the sound.	Colin says his head "ached."

3. Write a short summary of the reading, and tell what type of reading it is (fiction, poetry, etc.)

4. Your draft should contain:

- an introduction to the reading, including the title, author, and genre, or type (fiction, nonfiction, poetry)
- a brief summary of the reading
- your reaction to the reading (why you liked and disliked it)
- details to support your reaction
- an overall recommendation as to whether or not others would enjoy the reading

Writing: Create responses to literature: Demonstrate an understanding of the literary work, and support judgements through references to both the text and prior knowledge

Step Two: Practice Your Review

With a partner, take turns giving your reviews. Take notes about your partner's review. Is it clear? Does it give you a good idea of what the book is about? Does it make you want to read the book? Does it discourage you from reading the book?

Step Three: Present Your Review

Now you are ready to present your review to the rest of the class. Be prepared to answer questions about your review or your opinions.

Step Four: Evaluate Your Review

Ask your classmates whether or not your review made them want to read the selection. Use the Speaking Checklist to comment on each other's presentations.

Record Your Review

Record your presentation for a classroom listening lab. Listen to your own and others' recordings. Check out a speech to share at home or with another class.

Speaking Checklist

✔ Use appropriate tone of voice. Since a review is a persuasive presentation, your voice should be confident.

✔ Your pacing should be even throughout the presentation.

✔ Use your voice to emphasize the persuasive parts of your presentation.

✔ Speak slowly enough to be clear, especially when summarizing the plot.

✔ Try to make eye contact with members of your audience.

Reading: Read aloud fluently and accurately and with appropriate pacing, intonation, and expression

Write a Response to Literature: A Letter to a Friend

In Unit 4, you read about changes in people's lives. Such changes are often the central theme of literature. Choose the reading from Unit 4 that you feel most strongly about. This can be a reading that you really liked or disliked, or a reading that made you have a strong opinion. Then write a short letter to a friend that communicates what this reading makes you feel. Follow the steps below to plan and write your letter.

1. Pre-write

Brainstorm Write down the title of the reading on a blank piece of paper. Then, write your feelings about the reading and some reasons for your feelings, along with details from the story that they are connected to.

2. Draft

- Start your letter and write an opening paragraph

  Start your letter with the date and short greeting (for example: *Dear Justin*) and follow it with a comma. Then tell your friend that you read something that interested you, where you read it, and that you would like to tell him or her about it.

- Write about your feelings

  Tell your friend your feelings about the reading. Be sure to explain your feelings and to include details from the reading.

- Write a closing paragraph

  In a final paragraph, recommend the reading to your friend. Finish with a sentence about the next time you will meet.

3. Revise

Reread your draft and ask yourself these questions:

- Have I written the date at the top of my letter?

- Have I included a short greeting?

- Did I clearly express my thoughts and feelings about this reading?

- Did I add a closing and sign my letter?

  If you answered "No" to any of these questions, you will need to make changes to your letter to improve it. Work with a partner. Ask that person to

Writing: Write responses to literature: a. Develop an interpretation exhibiting careful reading, understanding, and insight; b. Organize the selected interpretation around several clear ideas, premises, or images; c. Develop and justify the selected interpretation through sustained use of examples and textual evidence

answer the same questions about your letter. Make any additional changes based on your partner's feedback.

4. Edit and Proofread

Proofread your revised letter. Check punctuation, capitalization, and spelling. Look in the dictionary to verify spelling. Correct any errors you find.

5. Publish

Now you are ready to publish your letter. Create a final version on a computer or word processor. Double-space your letter so that it is easier to read. Use the spell-checking tool to look for any misspelled words. Finally, be sure to write your name, date, teacher's name, and the name of your class at the top of the page. Here is an example of a published letter.

June 12, 2002

Dear Justin,

I just read a great story at school about a girl named Alma. I really liked it, and I think you'd like it, too. Let me tell you what I liked about it.

She had to change schools in the middle of fourth grade. So did I. I know how she felt. She had to sit in the back row, just because no one knew if she was a good student. That wasn't fair because later she moved up to the front row. But, she found a way to like her new place. She found a ballet school.

You are at a new school now. I think what Alma did will make you feel better. It's not long, and you'll like it. Then, next weekend when you come to visit, you can tell me what you think!

Your friend,

Dakota

Writing: Revise writing to improve the organization and consistency of ideas within and between paragraphs

Adventure Ads

Project Goal

In this unit, you read about new **adventures** and experiences. With a partner, you will create an **advertisement**, or ad. It should encourage one of the characters from the readings to try or buy something new.

1. With your partner, decide on a character. What type of new experience do you think he or she would be interested in? Travel or a cruise? A new hobby or computer?

2. Use magazines or the Internet to find ads. Do you think your character would be interested in any of these ads? Decide what you are going to **sell**.

3. On a poster board write your ad. Use **persuasive** words to encourage your character to try this out. Use words that would make your character buy what you are selling. Why might your character want or **need** this? Why might it be important to the character? Use the Internet to find pictures to illustrate your ad.

4. Show your ad to the class. See if your classmates can guess which character you have chosen.

Check Your Progress

Listening/Speaking: Did you explain your ad to the class?

Reading: Did you look back at the reading selections and think about the character you want to focus on?

Writing: Did you write a convincing advertisement?

Words to Know

advertisement
sell
persuasive
adventure
need

Writing: Write persuasive compositions: State a clear position, support the position with relevant information, and address reader concerns

hoose one or more of the following books to read. Write down in your Reading Log titles of the books you read and your opinion of each one. Ask yourself these questions.

1. What was the tone of this book? How did the author achieve this tone? (images, word choice, ideas)

2. Was this book written in first or third person?

3. How did this book develop the theme of passages?

4. Did you like the book? Why or why not? Give examples to support your opinion.

Nonfiction

A Year Down Yonder by Richard Peck
   A girl goes to live with her grandmother in a small town in rural Illinois.

Because of Winn-Dixie by Kate DiCamillo
   When a stray dog mysteriously appears in the local grocery store, India Opal Buloni's life changes.

Fiction

Hope Was Here by Joan Bauer
   Hope and her aunt move to a small town in Wisconsin to become waitresses at the Welcome Stairways Diner.

Joey Pigza Loses Control by Jack Gantos
   Joey spends the summer with a father he hardly knows. Although Joey has many hopes about their new life together, their lives soon get out of control.

Reading: Compare and contrast information on the same topic

Credits

ILLUSTRATIONS AND PHOTOGRAPHS

AFP/CORBIS: 144; Alan Flinn: 88, 89, 96, 97, 98, 99, 88, 108, 170, 175, 170; Ammann, Karl/CORBIS: 90, 92, 95; Amos, James L./CORBIS: 163; Belt, Annie Griffiths/CORBIS: 138; Bettmann/CORBIS: 63, 82, 112, 146, 191; Blair, Jonathan/CORBIS: 91; Cabib, Leila: 14, 16, 17, 162, 164; Carnegie Hero Fund: 79; Cha, Dia: 9; Conger, Dean/CORBIS: 127; Cooke, Jerry/CORBIS: 178; CORBIS: 81; David Diaz: icons; Dwight, Laura/CORBIS: 65; Ergenbright, Ric/CORBIS: 169; EyeWire: 54; Franz, D. Robert/CORBIS: 73; Garanger, Mark/CORBIS: 111; Gehman, Raymond/CORBIS: 45; Grossman, Myron: 22, 24, 26, 27, 28, 29, 30, 30, 118, 120, 121, 122, 123, 124, 125, 127; Gruen, John/CORBIS: 166; Gubb, Louise J./Image Works/Timepix: 80; Gulin, Darrell/CORBIS: 72; Hebberd, Lindsay/CORBIS: 66; Heinle & Heinle: 177; Hornak, Angelo/CORBIS: 193; Horner, Jeremy/CORBIS: 160; Johnson, Peter/CORBIS: 202, 203; Karr, Daniel: 43; Kelly-Mooney Photography/CORBIS: 168; Lepp, George/CORBIS: 72; Lerner Publications Group: 113; littlechiles.com: 17; Marshall, James/CORBIS: 140; Martin Rogers/CORBIS: 67; Maslen, Barbara: 108; Mason, Karen Huntt H./CORBIS: 94; Maze, Stephanie/CORBIS: 21; Michigan State University Museum: 13; Miller, Neal/Papilio/CORBIS: 192; Miyaki, Yoshi: 4, 7, 9, 76, 84, 85, 86; Mystic Aquarium: 145, 147; Ott, Kristi: 108, 109, 114, 115, 116, 117, 196, 199, 201; Perry, Clay/CORBIS: 194; Philbrook, Diana: 130, 131, 132, 133, 134, 135, 136, 137; PhotoDisk: 2, 6, 10, 15, 18, 20, 30, 31, 32, 33, 45, 44, 47, 64, 74, 75, 139, 152, 153, 167; Pollak, Barbara: 34, 37, 38, 39, 40, 41, 42, 43, 44, 46, 47; Price, Rick/CORBIS: 205; Raymer, Steve/CORBIS: 17; Rogers, Joel W./CORBIS: 195; Rothman, Jeffrey L./CORBIS: 142; Rowell, Galen/CORBIS: 204; Schermeister, Phil/CORBIS: 179; Scheuer, Lauren: 68, 70, 71; Schroeder, Glenn: 70; Schulke, Flip/CORBIS: 83; Simon & Schuster: 175; Smith, Richard Hamilton/CORBIS: 176; Souders, Paul A./CORBIS: 113; Swift, Chase/CORBIS: 46; Taylor, NJ: 150, 151, 180, 182, 183, 184, 185, 186, 187, 188, 189, 191; Vikander, Brian/CORBIS: 11; Watts, Ron/CORBIS: 106; Weinberg, Deirdre: 56, 58, 59, 60, 61, 62, 63; White. Ralph/CORBIS: 149.

AUTHORS

Unit 1: Changes

Pp. 6–9. "Dia's Story Cloth," text and illustrations copyright © 1996 by Denver Museum of Natural History. Permission arranged with Lee and Low Books, Inc., NY, NY 10016.

Pp. 16–17. "1. Angels Ride Bikes" and "2. Angels Ride Bikes." Reprinted with permission of the publisher, Children's Book Press, San Francisco, CA. *Angels Ride Bikes and Other Fall Poems/Los angeles andan en bicicleta y otros poemas de otoño.* Copyright © 1999 by Francisco X. Alarcon.

Pp. 24–26. "Death and the Afterlife," from *Ancient Egypt* by Judith Crosher, copyright © 1992 by Reed International Books, Ltd. Used by permission of Viking Penguin, an imprint of Penguin Putnam Books for Young Readers, a division of Penguin Putnam, Inc.

Pp. 27–29. "Recipe for a Mummy," from *Don't Try This at Home: Science Experiments for Kids on the Go* by Vicki Cobb. Copyright © 1998 by Vicki Cobb and Kathy Darling. Used by permission of HarperCollins Publishers.

Pp. 36–43. "The Great Turkey Walk," excerpt from *The Great Turkey Walk* by Kathleen Karr. Copyright © 1998 by Kathleen Karr. Reprinted with permission of Farrar, Straus and Giroux, LLC.

Unit 2: Heroes

Pp. 58–63. "The Big Friendly Giant" from *Danny: The Champion of the World* by Roald Dahl, copyright © 1975 by Roald Dahl. Used by permission by Alfred A. Knopf Children's Books, a division of Random House, Inc.

P. 70. "Hope," reprinted with the permission of Margaret K. McElderry Books, an imprint of Simon & Schuster Children's Publishing Division from *The Rainbow Hand* by Janet S. Wong. Copyright © 1999 Janet S. Wong.

P. 71. "When Tonya's Friends Come to Spend the Night," from *Night on Neighborhood Street* by Eloise Greenfield, copyright © 1991 by Eloise Greenfield. Used by permission of Dial Books for Young Readers, an imprint of Penguin Putnam Books for Young Readers, a division of Penguin Putnam, Inc.

Pp. 78–83. From *Who Cares? Millions Do . . . A Book about Altruism,* by Milton Meltzer, copyright © 1994, permission of Walker & Company, 435 Hudson St., New York, NY 10014.

Pp. 90–95. "A Conversation with Jane Goodall," from *Talking with Adventurers* by Pat Cummings and Linda Cummings, Ph.D., copyright © 1998 Jane Goodall. Reprinted with the permission of National Geographic Society Books.

Unit 3: Choices

Pp. 110–113. From *Avalanche* by Stephen Kramer. Copyright 1992 by Stephen Kramer. Published by Carolrhoda Books, Inc., a division of the Lerner Publishing Group. Used by permission of the publisher. All rights reserved.

Pp. 120–125. "Seventh Grade," from *Baseball in April and Other Stories* by Gary Soto. Copyright © 1990 by Gary Soto, reprinted by permission of Harcourt, Inc.

Pp. 132–137. From *Wringer* by Jerry Spinelli, copyright © 1997 by Jerry Spinelli. Used by permission of HarperCollins Publishers, Inc. Excerpts from pp. 88–93, 224–226.

Pp. 144–149. "A Conversation with Robert Ballard," from *Talking with Adventurers* by Pat Cummings and Linda Cummings, Ph.D., copyright © 1998 Robert Ballard. Reprinted with the permission of National Geographic Society Books.

Unit 4: Passages

P. 164. "Flowers," from *Angels* by Eloise Greenfield; drawing by Jan Spivey Gilchrist. Text copyright © 1998 by Eloise Greenfield. Reprinted by permission of Hyperion Books for Children.

Pp. 172–175. "Gilda," reprinted with permission of Atheneum Books for Young Readers, an imprint of Simon & Schuster Children's Publishing Division from *Under the Royal Palms* by Alma Flor Ada. Text copyright © 1998 by Alma Flor Ada.

Pp. 182–191. From *The Secret Garden,* by Frances Hodgson Burnett, illustrated by Russell Barnett, with line drawings by Sally Kindberg, Kaleidoscope Books. This edition Beehive Books, Orbis Publishing Ltd.

Pp. 198–201. Excerpt from *My Season with Penguins,* by Sophie Webb. Copyright © 2000 by Sophie Webb. Reprinted by permission of Houghton Mifflin Company. All rights reserved.

Index